EACL 2009 Workshop on the Interaction between Linguistics and Computational Linguistics: Virtuous, Vicious or Vacuous?

Held in Conjunction with EACL 2009

Athens, Greece
30 March 2009

ISBN: 978-1-61738-559-9

Printed from e-media with permission by:

Curran Associates, Inc.
57 Morehouse Lane
Red Hook, NY 12571
www.proceedings.com

Some format issues inherent in the e-media version may also appear in this print version.

Printed by Curran Associates, Inc. (2010)

Association for Computational Linguistics
209 N. Eighth Street
Stroudsburg, Pennsylvania 18360

Phone: 1-570-476-8006
Fax: 1-570-476-0860

acl@aclweb.org

Preface

This workshop is an attempt to bring together a range of linguists and computational linguists who operate across or near the computational "divide", to reflect on the relationship between the two fields, including the following questions:

- What contributions has computational linguistics made to linguistics, and vice versa?
- What are examples of success/failure of marrying linguistics and computational linguistics, and what can we learn from them?
- How can we better facilitate the virtuous cycle between computational linguistics and linguistics?
- Is modern-day computational linguistics relevant to current-day linguistics, and vice versa? If not, should it be made more relevant, and how?
- What do linguistics and computational linguistics stand to gain from greater cross-awareness between the two fields?
- What untapped areas/aspects of linguistics are ripe for cross-fertilisation with computational linguistics, and vice versa?

On the basis of exploring answers to these and other questions, the workshop aims to explore possible trajectories for linguistics and computational linguistics, in terms of both concrete low-level tasks and high-level aspirations/synergies.

In its infancy, computational linguistics drew heavily on theoretical linguistics. There have been numerous examples of co-development successes between computational and theoretical linguistics over the years (e.g. syntactic theories, discourse processing and language resource development), and significant crossover with other areas of linguistics such as psycholinguistics and corpus linguistics.

Throughout the history of the field, however, there has always been a subset of computational linguistics which has openly distanced itself from theoretical linguistics, perhaps most famously in the field of machine translation (MT) where there is relatively little in the majority of "successful" MT systems that a linguist would identify with. In the current climate of hard-core empiricism within computational linguistics it is appropriate to reflect on where we have come from and where we are headed relative to the various other fields of linguistics. As part of this reflection, it is timely to look beyond theoretical linguistics to the various other fields of linguistics which have traditionally received less exposure in computational linguistics, including sociolinguistics, historical linguistics, neurolinguistics and evolutionary linguistics.

We would like to thank all of our invited speakers and panelists for agreeing to participate in the workshop and help shape the debate. We would also like to thank the workshop chairs and local organisers of EACL 2009 for all of their behind-the-scenes efforts, without which this workshop would not have been possible. The workshop is endorsed by the Erasmus Mundus European Masters Program in Language and Communication Technologies (LCT; `http://lct-master.org`).

Timothy Baldwin
Valia Kordoni

Organizers

Workshop Chairs:

Timothy Baldwin, University of Melbourne (Australia)
Valia Kordoni, DFKI and Saarland University (Germany)

Invited Speakers:

Mark Johnson, Brown University (USA)
Frank Keller, University of Edinburgh (UK)
Mark Liberman, University of Pennsylvania (USA)
Stelios Piperidis, Institute for Language and Speech Processing (Greece)
Geoffrey Pullum, University of Edinburgh (UK)

Panelists:

Emily Bender, University of Washington (USA)
Gregor Erbach, European Union (Belgium)
Bob Moore, Microsoft Research (USA)
Gertjan van Noord, University of Groningen (Netherlands)
Hans Uszkoreit, DFKI and Saarland University (Germany)

Table of Contents

Machine Translation and its Philosophical Accounts
Stelios Piperidis 1

The Annotation Conundrum
Mark Liberman 2

How the Statistical Revolution Changes (Computational) Linguistics
Mark Johnson 3

Computational Linguistics and Generative Linguistics: The Triumph of Hope over Experience
Geoffrey Pullum 12

Linguistics in Computational Linguistics: Observations and Predictions
Hans Uszkoreit 22

Linguistically Naïve != Language Independent: Why NLP Needs Linguistic Typology
Emily M. Bender 26

Parsed Corpora for Linguistics
Gertjan van Noord and Gosse Bouma 33

Computational Linguistics and Linguistics: What Keeps Them together, What Sets Them apart?
Gregor Erbach 40

What Do Computational Linguists Need to Know about Linguistics?
Robert C. Moore 41

The Interaction of Syntactic Theory and Computational Psycholinguistics
Frank Keller 43

Workshop Program

Monday, March 30, 2009

8:55–9:00 Opening Remarks

09:00-09:45 *Machine Translation and its Philosophical Accounts*
Stelios Piperidis

09:45-10:30 *The Annotation Conundrum*
Mark Liberman

10:30-11:00 Coffee Break

11:00-11:45 *How the Statistical Revolution Changes (Computational) Linguistics*
Mark Johnson

11:45-12:30 Discussion

12:30-14:00 Lunch Break

14:00-14:45 *Computational Linguistics and Generative Linguistics: The Triumph of Hope over Experience*
Geoffrey Pullum

14:45-16:00 Panel and Discussion

Linguistics in Computational Linguistics: Observations and Predictions
Hans Uszkoreit

Linguistically Naïve != Language Independent: Why NLP Needs Linguistic Typology
Emily M. Bender

Parsed Corpora for Linguistics
Gertjan van Noord and Gosse Bouma

Computational Linguistics and Linguistics: What Keeps Them together, What Sets Them apart?
Gregor Erbach

What Do Computational Linguists Need to Know about Linguistics?
Robert C. Moore

16:00-16:30 Coffee Break

Monday, March 30, 2009 (continued)

16:30-17:15	*The Interaction of Syntactic Theory and Computational Psycholinguistics* Frank Keller
17:15-17:55	Discussion
17:55-18:00	Closing Remarks

Machine Translation and its philosophical accounts

Stelios Piperidis
Institute for Language and Speech Processing,
"Athena" Research Centre
spip@ilsp.gr

Abstract

This paper attempts to explore the interrelation between philosophical accounts of language and respective technological developments in the field of human language technologies. In doing so, it focuses on the interaction between analytical philosophy and machine translation development, trying to draw the emerging methodological analogies.

1 Introduction

Philosophical accounts of science and respective technological development bear a tight interrelation and continuous interplay. Likewise, philosophical investigations of language bear their own implications on how technology processing language, in monolingual or multilingual settings, evolves.

In the multilingual setting, machine translation feasibility, its presuppositions and implications, brings forth a range of questions, applicable to human translation as well, including, but not limited to, linguistic and ontological relativity, indeterminacy of translation, inscrutability of reference, representational function of language, the problem of meaning.

Bar Hillel's claims on the infeasibility of machine translation and the Sapir-Whorf hypothesis with the linguistic determinism and relativity principles, partly backed up by Quine's ontological relativity and later Wittgenstein's private language and variability of language games have haunted the way of thinking in machine translation development. Indeterminacy, relativity, and the consequent abolition of the one gold translation idea, however, as well as the necessity for frameworks integrating pragmatic and behavioural data in translation have played their role in advancing machine translation design paving the way for observed paradigm shifts at all stages of development.

In broadly dividing machine translation history in the rule-based and corpus-based eras, in the 50's and 80's respectively, one can draw the analogies that would rather point to a tight interaction between philosophical accounts and machine translation paradigms.

Early contemporary analytic philosophy, through conceptual, reference-bound analysis and compositionality principles, provided the foundation for representational, rule and knowledge-based approaches of early machine translation, from 50's through the 80's. The turn, in analytic philosophy, to an understanding of meaning though use, to pragmatics and behaviourism, may be paired and seen as laying the foundation for the machine translation paradigm shift observed in the 80's. In this pairing, it is the use of the much required parallel (or comparable) translation data that could be seen as constituting the behavioural data base, with each alignment function being conceived of as the result of a radical translation process, where a source language sentence provides the sensory data and a target language sentence provides the linguistic observation. In such a framework, this aligned data source does provide the "translation manual", which after a series of inductive operations does converge to a potentially usable set of translation relations.

Along this line, we will discuss, in this talk, the continuous relations between analytic philosophy, linguistic science and human language technologies. Such relations, direct or indirect, can be bi-directional and can possibly work towards better understanding and facilitating the virtuous cycle between language technology and its theoretical underpinnings.

Proceedings of the EACL 2009 Workshop on the Interaction between Linguistics and Computational Linguistics, page 1,
Athens, Greece, 30 March, 2009. ©2009 Association for Computational Linguistics

The Annotation Conundrum

Mark Liberman
University of Pennsylvania
myl@cis.upenn.edu

Abstract

Without lengthy, iterative refinement of guidelines, and equally lengthy and iterative training of annotators, the level of inter-subjective agreement on simple tasks of phonetic, phonological, syntactic, semantic, and pragmatic annotation is shockingly low.

This is a significant practical problem in speech and language technology, but it poses questions of interest to psychologists, philosophers of language, and theoretical linguists as well.

1 Introduction

Biologists believe that they know what genes, organisms, chemical compounds, and diseases are. Linguists believe that they know what nouns, verbs, and clauses are. Ordinary literate speakers of English believe that they know what people, places, and organizations are. And all of them believe that they can recognize and understand instances of these categories in coherent text.

When two biologists, two linguists, or two English speakers discuss such texts, it seems plausible that they have understood such instances in the same way. Nevertheless, if they are asked to highlight these instances, the level of inter-subjective agreement will be shockingly low.

Similarly depressing results are obtained in tasks such as phonetic or surface-phonemic transcription, co-reference annotation, identification of animacy, etc. Things are usually not much better if we compare annotations produced by the same individuals on different occasions.

A solution exists, in the practical sense of producing annotations with high inter-annotator agreement scores. The initially-divergent results of multiple annotations are discussed and adjudicated, and principles of interpretation are defined for future use. This process is repeated over and over again, typically for several months, until the desired level of agreement is obtained, or funding runs out.

At least for simple linguistic annotation tasks, this process, reminiscent of the development of common law, generally converges (though the residual level of disagreement may be depressingly high, especially when multiple judgments must be cascaded). The resulting annotation manuals may be hundreds of pages long, even for fairly limited tasks; and new annotators face weeks or months of training to become competent in learning to apply them.

There are several obvious ideas about why this might be true, but most of these ideas seem to be false. It will be argued that part of the answer lies in understanding that most linguistic annotation tasks are not really classification problems, but rather translation problems. We don't normally assume that there is only one correct translation of a Chinese sentence into English; nor do we try to make this true by constructing elaborate translation guidelines to cover every relevant contingency, though in principle we could.

Implications in engineering and science will be discussed.

Proceedings of the EACL 2009 Workshop on the Interaction between Linguistics and Computational Linguistics, page 2,
Athens, Greece, 30 March, 2009. ©2009 Association for Computational Linguistics

How the statistical revolution changes (computational) linguistics

Mark Johnson
Cognitive and Linguistic Sciences and Computer Science
Brown University
Mark_Johnson@Brown.edu

Abstract

This paper discusses some of the ways that the "statistical revolution" has changed and continues to change the relationship between linguistics and computational linguistics. I claim that it is more useful in parsing to make an open world assumption about possible linguistic structures, rather than the closed world assumption usually made in grammar-based approaches to parsing, and I sketch two different ways in which grammar-based approaches might be modified to achieve this. I also describe some of the ways in which probabilistic models are starting to have a significant impact on psycholinguistics and language acquisition. In language acquisition Bayesian techniques may let us empirically evaluate the role of putative universals in universal grammar.

1 Introduction

The workshop organizers asked us to write something controversial to stimulate discussion, and I've attempted to do that here. Usually in my papers I try to stick to facts and claims that I can support, but here I have fearlessly and perhaps foolishly gone out on a limb and presented guesses, hunches and opinions. Take them with a grain of salt. Inspired by Wanamaker's well-known quote about advertising, I expect that half of the ideas I'm proposing here are wrong, but I don't know which half. I hope the conference will help me figure that out.

Statistical techniques have revolutionized many scientific fields in the past two decades, including computational linguistics. This paper discusses the impact of this on the relationship between computational linguistics and linguistics. I'm presenting a personal perspective rather than a scientific review here, and for this reason I focus on areas I have some experience with. I begin by discussing how the statistical perspective changed my understanding of the relationship between linguistic theory, grammars and parsing, and then go on to describe some of the ways that ideas from statistics and machine learning are starting to have an impact on linguistics today.

Before beginning, I'd like to say something about what I think computational linguistics is. I view computational linguistics as having both a scientific and an engineering side. The engineering side of computational linguistics, often called natural language processing (NLP), is largely concerned with building computational tools that do useful things with language, e.g., machine translation, summarization, question-answering, etc. Like any engineering discipline, natural language processing draws on a variety of different scientific disciplines.

I think it's fair to say that in the current state of the art, natural language processing draws far more heavily on statistics and machine learning than it does on linguistic theory. For example, one might claim that all an NLP engineer really needs to understand about linguistic theory are (say) the parts of speech (POS). Assuming this is true (I'm not sure it is), would it indicate that there is something wrong with either linguistic theory or computational linguistics? I don't think it does: there's no reason to expect an engineering solution to utilize all the scientific knowledge of a related field. The fact that you can build perfectly good bridges with Newtonian mechanics says nothing about the truth of quantum mechanics.

I also believe that there is a scientific field of computational linguistics. This scientific field exists not just because computers are incredibly useful for doing linguistics — I expect that computers have revolutionized most fields of science — but because it makes sense to think of linguis-

Proceedings of the EACL 2009 Workshop on the Interaction between Linguistics and Computational Linguistics, pages 3–11,
Athens, Greece, 30 March, 2009. ©2009 Association for Computational Linguistics

tic *processes* as being essentially computational in nature. If we take computation to be the manipulation of symbols in a meaning-respecting way, then it seems reasonable to hypothesize that language comprehension, production and acquisition are all computational processes. Viewed this way, we might expect computational linguistics to interact most strongly with those areas of linguistics that study linguistic processing, namely psycholinguistics and language acquisition. As I explain in section 3 below, I think we are starting to see this happen.

2 Grammar-based and statistical parsing

In some ways the 1980s were a golden age for collaboration and cross-fertilization between linguistic theory and computational linguistics, especially between syntax and parsing. Gazdar and colleagues showed that Chomskyian transformations could be supplanted by computationally much simpler feature passing mechanisms (Gazdar et al., 1985), and this lead to an explosion of work on "unification-based" grammars (Shieber, 1986), including the Lexical-Functional Grammars and Head-driven Phrase Structure Grammars that are still very actively pursued today. I'll call the work on parsing within this general framework the *grammar-based approach* in order to contrast it with the *statistical approach* that doesn't rely on these kinds of grammars. I think the statistical approach has come to dominate computational linguistics, and in this section I'll describe why this happened.

Before beginning I think it's useful to clarify our goals for building parsers. There are many reasons why one might build any computational system — perhaps it's a part of a commercial product we hope will make us rich, or perhaps we want to test the predictions of a certain theory of processing — and these reasons should dictate how and even whether the system is constructed. I'm assuming in this section that we want to build parsers because we expect the representations they produce will be useful for various other NLP engineering tasks. This means that parser design is itself essentially an engineering task, i.e., we want a device that returns parses that are accurate as possible for as many sentences as possible.

I'll begin by discussing a couple of differences between the approaches that are often mentioned but I don't think are really that important. The grammar-based approaches are sometimes described as producing deeper representations that are closer to meaning. It certainly is true that grammar-based analyses typically represent predicate-argument structure and perhaps also quantifier scope. But one can recover predicate-argument structure using statistical methods (see the work on semantic role labeling and "PropBank" parsing (Palmer et al., 2005)), and presumably similar methods could be used to resolve quantifier scope as well.

I suspect the main reason why statistical parsing has concentrated on more superficial syntactic structure (such as phrase structure) is because there aren't many actual applications for the syntactic analyses our parsers return. Given the current state-of-the-art in knowledge representation and artificial intelligence, even if we could produce completely accurate logical forms in some higher-order logic, it's not clear whether we could do anything useful with them. It's hard to find real applications that benefit from even syntactic information, and the information any such applications actually use is often fairly superficial. For example, some research systems for named entity detection and extraction use parsing to identify noun phrases (which are potentially name entities) as well as the verbs that govern them, but they ignore the rest of the syntactic structure. In fact, many applications of statistical parsers simply use them as language models, i.e., one parses to obtain the probability that the parser assigns to the string and throws away the parses it computes in the process (Jelinek, 2004). (It seems that such parsing-based language models are good at preferring strings that are at least superficially grammatical, e.g., where each clause contains one verb phrase, which is useful in applications such as summarization and machine translation).

Grammar-based approaches are also often described as more linguistically based, while statistical approaches are viewed as less linguistically informed. I think this view primarily reflects the origins of the two approaches: the grammar-based approach arose from the collaboration between linguists and computer scientists in the 1980s mentioned earlier, while the statistical approach has its origins in engineering work in speech recognition in which linguists did not play a major role. I also think this view is basically false. In the grammar-based approaches linguists write the grammars while in statistical approaches linguists annotate the corpora with syntactic parses, so linguists play a central role in both. (It's an interesting question as to why corpus annotation plus statistical inference seems to be a more effective way of getting linguistic information into a computer than manually writing a grammar).

Rather, I think that computational linguists working on statistical parsing need a greater level of linguistic sensitivity at an informal level than those working on grammar-based approaches. In the grammar-based approaches all linguistic knowledge is contained in the grammar, which the computational linguist implementing the parsing framework doesn't actually have to understand. All she has to do is correctly implement an inference engine for grammars written in the relevant grammar formalism. By contrast, statistical parsers define the probability of a parse in terms of its (statistical) features or properties, and a parser designer needs to choose which features their parser will use, and many of these features reflect at least an intuitive understanding of linguistic dependencies. For example, statistical parsers from Magerman (1995) on use features based on head-dependent relationships. (The parsers developed by the Berkeley group are a notable exception (Petrov and Klein, 2007)). While it's true that only a small fraction of our knowledge about linguistic structure winds up expressed by features in modern statistical parsers, as discussed above there's no reason to expect all of our scientific knowledge to be relevant to any engineering problem. And while many of the features used in statistical parsers don't correspond to linguistic constraints, nobody seriously claims that humans understand language only using linguistic constraints of the kind expressed in formal grammars. I suspect that many of the features that have been shown to be useful in statistical parsing encode psycholinguistic markedness preferences (e.g., attachment preferences) and at least some aspects of world knowledge (e.g., that the direct object of "eat" is likely to be a food).

Moreover, it's not necessary for a statistical model to exactly replicate a linguistic constraint in order for it to effectively capture the corresponding generalization: all that's necessary is that the statistical features "cover" the relevant examples. For example, adding a subject-verb agreement feature to the Charniak-Johnson parser (Charniak and Johnson, 2005) has no measurable effect on parsing accuracy. After doing this experiment I realized this shouldn't be surprising: the Charniak parser already conditions each argument's part-of-speech (POS) on its governor's POS, and since POS tags distinguish singular and plural nouns and verbs, these general head-argument POS features capture most cases of subject-verb agreement.

Note that I'm not claiming that subject-verb agreement isn't a real linguistic constraint or that it doesn't play an important role in human parsing. I think that the type of input (e.g., treebanks) and the kinds of abilities (e.g., to exactly count the occurences of many different constructions) available to our machines may be so different to what is available to a child that the features that work best in our parsers need not bear much relationship to those used by humans.

Still, I view the design of the features used in statistical parsers as a fundamentally linguistic issue (albeit one with computational consequences, since the search problem in parsing is largely determined by the features involved), and I expect there is still more to learn about which combinations of features are most useful for statistical parsing. My guess is that the features used in e.g., the Collins (2003) or Charniak (2000) parsers are probably close to optimal for English Penn Treebank parsing (Marcus et al., 1993), but that other features might improve parsing of other languages or even other English genres. Unfortunately changing the features used in these parsers typically involves significant reprogramming, which makes it difficult for linguists to experiment with new features. However, it might be possible to develop a kind of statistical parsing framework that makes it possible to define new features and integrate them into a statistical parser without any programming which would make it easy to explore novel combinations of statistical features; see Goodman (1998) for an interesting suggestion along these lines.

From a high-level perspective, the grammar-based approaches and the statistical approaches both view parsing fundamentally in the same way, namely as a specialized kind of inference problem. These days I view "parsing as deduction" (one of the slogans touted by the grammar-based crowd) as unnecessarily restrictive; after all, psycholinguistic research shows that humans are exquisitely sensitive to distributional information, so why shouldn't we let our parsers use that information as well? And as Abney (1997) showed, it is mathematically straight-forward to define probability distributions over the representations used by virtually any theory of grammar (even those of Chomsky's Minimalism), which means that theoretically the arsenal of statistical methods for parsing and learning can be applied to any grammar just as well.

In the late 1990s I explored these kinds of statistical models for Lexical-Functional Grammar (Bresnan, 1982; Johnson et al., 1999). The hope was that statistical features based on LFG's richer representations (specifically, f-structures) might result in better parsing accuracy. However, this seems not to be the case. As mentioned above, Abney's formulation of probabilistic models makes essentially no demands on what linguistic representations actually are; all that is required is that the statistical features are functions that map each representation to a real number. These are used to map a set of linguistic representations (say, the set of all grammatical analyses) to a set of vectors of real numbers. Then by defining a distribution over these sets of real-valued vectors we implicitly define a distribution over the corresponding linguistic representations.

This means that as far as the probabilistic model is concerned the details of the linguistic representations don't actually matter, so long as there are the right number of them and it is possible to compute the necessary real-valued vectors from them. For a computational linguist this is actually quite a liberating point of view; we aren't restricted to slavishly reproducing textbook linguistic structures, but are free to experiment with alternative representations that might have computational or other advantages.

In my case, it turned out that the kinds of features that were most useful for stochastic LFG parsing could in fact be directly computed from phrase-structure trees. The features that involved f-structure properties could be covered by other features defined directly on the phrase-structure trees. (Some of these phrase-structure features were implemented by rather nasty C++ routines but that doesn't matter; Abney-type models make no assumptions about what the feature functions are). This meant that I didn't actually need the f-structures to define the probability distributions I was interested in; all I needed were the corresponding c-structure or phrase-structure trees.

And of course there are many ways of obtaining phrase-structure trees. At the time my colleague Eugene Charniak was developing a statistical phrase-structure parser that was more robust and had broader coverage than the LFG parser I was working with, and I found I generally got better performance if I used the trees his parser produced, so that's what I did. This leads to the discriminative re-ranking approach developed by Collins and Koo (2005), in which a statistical parser trained on a treebank is used to produce a set of candidate parses which are then "re-ranked" by an Abney-style probabilistic model.

I suspect these robustness and coverage problems of grammar-based parsing are symptoms of a fundamental problem in the standard way that grammar-based parsing is understood. First, I think grammar-based approaches face a dilemma: on the one hand the explosion of ambiguity suggests that some sentences get too many parses, while the problems of coverage show that some sentences get too few, i.e., zero, parses. While it's possible that there is a single grammar that can resolve this dilemma, my point here is that each of these problems suggests we need to modify the grammars in exactly the opposite way, i.e., generally tighten the constraints in order to reduce ambiguity, while generally relax the constraints in order to allow more parses for sentences that have no parses at all.

Second, I think this dilemma only arises because the grammar-based approach to parsing is fundamentally designed around the goal of distinguishing grammatical from ungrammatical sentences. While I agree with Pullum (2007) that grammaticality is and should be central to syntactic theory, I suspect it is not helpful to view parsing (by machines or humans) as a byproduct of proving the grammaticality of a sentence. In most of the applications I can imagine, what we really want from a parser is the parse that reflects its best guess at the intended interpretation of the input, even if that input is ungrammatical. For example, given the telegraphese input "man bites dog" we want the parser to tell us that "man" is likely to be the agent of "bites" and "dog" the patient, and not simply that the sentence is ungrammatical.

These grammars typically distinguish grammatical from ungrammatical analyses by explicitly characterizing the set of grammatical analyses in some way, and then assuming that all other analyses are ungrammatical. Borrowing terminology from logic programming (Lloyd, 1987) we might call this a *closed-world assumption*: any analysis the grammar does not generate is assumed to be ungrammatical.

Interestingly, I think that the probabilistic models used statistical parsing generally make an *open-world assumption* about linguistic analyses. These probabilistic models prefer certain linguistic structures over others, but the smoothing mechanisms that these methods use ensure that every possible analysis (and hence every possible string) receives positive probability. In such an approach the statistical features identify properties of syntactic analyses which make the analysis more or less likely, so the probabilistic model can prefer, disprefer or simply be ambivalent about any particular linguistic feature or construction.

I think an open-world assumption is generally preferable as a model of syntactic parsing in both humans and machines. I think it's not reasonable to assume that the parser knows all the lexical entries and syntactic constructions of the language it is parsing. Even if the parser encounters a word or construction it doesn't understand it, that shouldn't stop it from interpreting the rest of the sentence. Statistical parsers are considerably more open-world. For example, unknown words don't present any fundamental problem for statistical parsers; in the absence of specific lexical information about a word they automatically back off to generic information about words in general.

Does the closed-world assumption inherent in the standard approach to grammar-based parsing mean we have to abandon it? I don't think so; I can imagine at least two ways in which the conventional grammar-based approach might be modified to obtain an open-world parsing model.

One possible approach keeps the standard closed-world conception that grammars generate only grammatical analyses, but gives up the idea that parsing is a byproduct of determining the grammaticality of the input sentence. Instead, we might use a *noisy channel* to map grammatical analyses generated by the grammar to the actual input sentences we have to parse. Parsing involves recovering the grammatical source or underlying sentence as well as its structure. Presumably the channel model would be designed to prefer minimal distortion, so if the input to be parsed is in fact grammatical then the channel would prefer the identity transformation, while if the input is ungrammatical the channel model would map it to close grammatical sentences. For example, if such a parser were given the input "man bites dog" it might decide that the most probable underlying sentence is "a man bites a dog" and return a parse for that sentence. Such an approach might be regarded as a way of formalizing the idea that ungrammatical sentences are interpreted by analogy with grammatical ones. (Charniak and I proposed a noisy channel model along these lines for parsing transcribed speech (Johnson and Charniak, 2004)).

Another possible approach involves modifying our interpretation of the grammar itself. We could obtain an open world model by relaxing our interpretation of some or all of the constraints in the grammar. Instead of viewing them as hard constraints that define a set of grammatical constructions, we reinterpret them as violable, probabilistic features. For example, instead of interpreting subject-verb agreement as a hard constraint that rules out certain syntactic analyses, we reinterpret it as a soft constraint that penalizes analyses in which subject-verb agreement fails. Instead of assuming that each verb comes with a fixed set of subcategorization requirements, we might view subcategorization as preferences for certain kinds of complements, implemented by features in an Abney-style statistical model. Unknown words come with no subcategorization preferences of their own, so they would inherit the prior or default preferences. Formally, I think this is fairly easy to achieve: we replace the hard unification constraints (e.g., that the subject's number feature equals the verb's number feature) with a stochastic feature that fires whenever the subject's number feature differs from the verb's number feature, and rely on the statistical model training procedure to estimate that feature's weight.

Computationally, I suspect that either of these options (or any other option that makes the grammar-based approaches open world) will require a major rethinking of the parsing process. Notice that both approaches let ambiguity proliferate (ambiguity is our friend in the fight against poor coverage), so we would need parsing algorithms capable of handling massive ambiguity. This is true of most statistical parsing models, so it is possible that the same approaches that have proven successful in statistical parsing (e.g., using probabilities to guide search, dynamic programming, coarse-to-fine) will be useful here as well.

3 Statistical models and linguistics

The previous section focused on syntactic parsing, which is an area in which there's been a fruitful interaction between linguistic theory and computational linguistics over a period of several decades. In this section I want to discuss two other emerging areas in which I expect the interaction between linguistics and computational linguistics to become increasingly important: psycholinguistics and language acquisition. I think it's no accident that these areas both study processing (rather than an area of theoretical linguistics such as syntax or semantics), since I believe that the scientific side of computational linguistics is fundamentally about such linguistic processes.

Just to be clear: psycholinguistics and language acquisition are experimental disciplines, and I don't expect the average researcher in those fields to start doing computational linguistics any time soon. However, I do think there are an emerging cadre of young researchers in both fields applying ideas and results from computational linguistics in their work and using experimental results from their field to develop and improve the computational models. For example, in psycholinguistics researchers such as Hale (2006) and Levy (2008) are using probabilistic models of syntactic structure to make predictions about human sentence processing, and Bachrach (2008) is using predictions from the Roark (2001) parser to help explain the patterns of fMRI activation observed during sentence comprehension. In the field of language acquisition computational linguists such as Klein and Manning (2004) have studied the unsupervised acquisition of syntactic structure, while linguists such as Boersma and Hayes (2001), Goldsmith (2001), Pater (2008) and Albright and Hayes (2003) are developing probabilistic models of the acquisition of phonology and/or morphology, and Frank et al. (2007) experimentally tests the predictions of a Bayesian model of lexical acquisition. Since I have more experience with computational models of language acquisition, I'll concentrate on this topic for the rest of this section.

Much of this work can be viewed under the slogan "structured statistical learning". That is, specifying the structures over which the learning algorithm generalizes is just as important as specifying the learning algorithm itself. One of the things I like about this work is that it gets beyond the naive nature-versus-nurture arguments that characterize some of the earlier theoretical work on language acquisition. Instead, these computational models become tools for investigating the effect of specific structural assumptions on the acquisition process. For example, Goldwater et al. (2007) shows that modeling inter-word dependencies improves word segmentation, which shows that the linguistic context contains information that is potentially very useful for lexical acquisition.

I think it's no accident that much of the computational work is concerned with phonology and morphology. These fields seem to be closer to the data and the structures involved seem simpler than in, say, syntax and semantics. I suspect that linguists working in phonology and morphology find it easier to understand and accept probabilistic models in large part because of Smolensky's work on Optimality Theory (Smolensky and Legendre, 2005). Smolensky found a way of introducing optimization into linguistic theory in a way that linguists could understand, and this serves as a very important bridge for them to probabilistic models.

As I argued above, it's important with any computational modeling to be clear about exactly what our computational models are intended to achieve. Perhaps the most straight-forward goal for computational models of language acquisition is to view them as specifying the actual computations that a human performs when learning a language. Under this conception we expect the computational model to describe the learning trajectory of language acquisition, e.g., if it takes the algorithm more iterations to learn one word than another, then we would expect humans to take longer to that word as well. Much of the work in computational phonology seems to take this perspective (Boersma and Hayes, 2001).

Alternatively, we might view our probabilistic models (rather than the computational procedures that implementing them) as embodying the scientific claims we want to make. Because these probabilistic models are too complex to analyze analytically in general we need a computational procedure to compute the model's predictions, but the computational procedure itself is not claimed to have any psychological reality. For example, we might claim that the grammar a child will learn is the one that is optimal with respect to a certain probabilistic model. We need an algorithm for computing this optimal grammar so we can check the probabilistic model's predictions and to convince ourselves we're not expecting the learner to perform magic, but we might not want to claim that humans use this algorithm. To use terminology from the grammar-based approaches mentioned earlier, a probabilistic model is a *declarative specification* of the distribution of certain variables, but it says nothing about how this distribution might actually be calculated. I think Marr's "three levels" capture this difference nicely: the question is whether we take our models to be "algorithmic level" or "computational level" descriptions of cognitive processes (Marr, 1982).

Looking into the future, I'm very excited about Bayesian approaches to language acquisition, as I think they have the potential to let us finally examine deep questions about language acquisition in a quantitative way. The Bayesian approach factors learning problems into two pieces: the likelihood and the prior. The likelihood encodes the information obtained from the data, while the prior encodes the information possessed by the learner before learning commences (Pearl, 1988). In principle the prior can encode virtually any information, including information claimed to be part of universal grammar.

Bayesian priors can incorporate the properties linguists often take to be part of universal grammar, such as X' theory. A Bayesian prior can also express soft markedness preferences as well as hard constraints. Moreover, the prior can also incorporate preferences that are not specifically linguistic, such as a preference for shorter grammars or smaller lexicons, i.e., the kinds of preferences sometimes expressed by an evaluation metric (Chomsky, 1965).

The Bayesian framework therefore provides us with a tool to quantitatively evaluate the impact of different purported linguistic universals on language acquisition. For example, we can calculate the contribution of, say, hypothetical X' theory universals on the acquisition of syntax. The Bayesian framework is flexible enough to also permit us to evaluate the contribution of the non-linguistic context on learning (Frank et al., to appear). Finally, non-parametric Bayesian methods permit us to learn models with an unbounded number features, perhaps giving us the mathematical and computational tools to understand the induction of rules and complex structure (Johnson et al., 2007).

Of course doing this requires developing actual Bayesian models of language, and this is not easy. Even though this research is still just beginning, it's clear that the details of the models have a huge impact on how well they work. It's not enough to "assume some version of X' theory"; one needs to evaluate specific proposals. Still, my hope is that being able to evaluate the contributions of specific putative universals may help us measure and understand their contributions (if any) to the learning process.

4 Conclusion

In this paper I focused on two areas of interaction between computational linguistics and linguistic theory. In the area of parsing I argued that we should design parsers so they incorporate an open-world assumption about sentences and their linguistic structures and sketched two ways in which grammar-based approaches might be modified to make them do this; both of which involve abandoning the idea that parsing is solely a process of proving the grammaticality of the input.

Then I discussed how probabilistic models are being applied in the fields of sentence processing and language acquisition. Here I believe we're at the beginning of a very fruitful period of interaction between empirical research and computational modeling, with insights and results flowing both ways.

But what does all this mean for mainstream computational linguistics? Can we expect theoretical linguistics to play a larger role in computational linguistics in the near future? If by computational linguistics we mean the NLP engineering applications that typically receive the bulk of the attention at today's Computational Linguistics conferences, I'm not so sure. While it's reasonable to expect that better scientific theories of how humans understand language will help us build better computational systems that do the same, I think we should remember that our machines can do things that no human can (e.g., count all the 5-grams in terabytes of data), and so our engineering solutions may differ considerably from the algorithms and procedures used by humans. But I think it's also reasonable to hope that the interdisciplinary work involving statistics, computational models, psycholinguistics and language acquisition that I mentioned in the paper will produce new insights into how language is acquired and used.

Acknowledgments

I'd like to thank Eugene Charniak and Antske Fokkens for stimulating discussion and helpful comments on an earlier draft. Of course all opinions expressed here are my own.

References

Steven Abney. 1997. Stochastic Attribute-Value Grammars. *Computational Linguistics*, 23(4):597–617.

A. Albright and B. Hayes. 2003. Rules vs. analogy in English past tenses: a computational/experimental study. *Cognition*, 90:118–161.

Asaf Bachrach. 2008. *Imaging Neural Correlates of Syntactic Complexity in a Naturalistic Context*. Ph.D. thesis, Massachusetts Institute of Technology, Cambridge, Massachusetts.

P. Boersma and B. Hayes. 2001. Empirical tests of the gradual learning algorithm. *Linguistic Inquiry*, 32(1):45–86.

Joan Bresnan. 1982. Control and complementation. In Joan Bresnan, editor, *The Mental Representation of Grammatical Relations*, pages 282–390. The MIT Press, Cambridge, Massachusetts.

Eugene Charniak and Mark Johnson. 2005. Coarse-to-fine n-best parsing and MaxEnt discriminative reranking. In *Proceedings of the 43rd Annual Meeting of the Association for Computational Linguistics*, pages 173–180, Ann Arbor, Michigan, June. Association for Computational Linguistics.

Eugene Charniak. 2000. A maximum-entropy-inspired parser. In *The Proceedings of the North American Chapter of the Association for Computational Linguistics*, pages 132–139.

Noam Chomsky. 1965. *Aspects of the Theory of Syntax*. The MIT Press, Cambridge, Massachusetts.

Michael Collins and Terry Koo. 2005. Discriminative reranking for natural language parsing. *Computational Linguistics*, 31(1):25–70.

Michael Collins. 2003. Head-driven statistical models for natural language parsing. *Computational Linguistics*, 29(4):589–638.

Michael C. Frank, Sharon Goldwater, Vikash Mansinghka, Tom Griffiths, and Joshua Tenenbaum. 2007. Modeling human performance on statistical word segmentation tasks. In *Proceedings of the 29th Annual Meeting of the Cognitive Science Society*.

Michael C. Frank, Noah Goodman, and Joshua Tenenbaum. to appear. Using speakers referential intentions to model early cross-situational word learning. *Psychological Science*.

Gerald Gazdar, Ewan Klein, Geoffrey Pullum, and Ivan Sag. 1985. *Generalized Phrase Structure Grammar*. Basil Blackwell, Oxford.

J. Goldsmith. 2001. Unsupervised learning of the morphology of a natural language. *Computational Linguistics*, 27:153–198.

Sharon Goldwater, Thomas L. Griffiths, and Mark Johnson. 2007. Distributional cues to word boundaries: Context is important. In David Bamman, Tatiana Magnitskaia, and Colleen Zaller, editors, *Proceedings of the 31st Annual Boston University Conference on Language Development*, pages 239–250, Somerville, MA. Cascadilla Press.

J. Goodman. 1998. *Parsing inside-out*. Ph.D. thesis, Harvard University. available from http://research.microsoft.com/~joshuago/.

John Hale. 2006. Uncertainty about the rest of the sentence. *Cognitive Science*, 30:643–672.

Fred Jelinek. 2004. Stochastic analysis of structured language modeling. In Mark Johnson, Sanjeev P. Khudanpur, Mari Ostendorf, and Roni Rosenfeld, editors, *Mathematical Foundations of Speech and Language Processing*, pages 37–72. Springer, New York.

Mark Johnson and Eugene Charniak. 2004. A TAG-based noisy channel model of speech repairs. In *Proceedings of the 42nd Annual Meeting of the Association for Computational Linguistics*, pages 33–39.

Mark Johnson, Stuart Geman, Stephen Canon, Zhiyi Chi, and Stefan Riezler. 1999. Estimators for stochastic "unification-based" grammars. In *The Proceedings of the 37th Annual Conference of the Association for Computational Linguistics*, pages 535–541, San Francisco. Morgan Kaufmann.

Mark Johnson, Thomas L. Griffiths, and Sharon Goldwater. 2007. Adaptor Grammars: A framework for specifying compositional nonparametric Bayesian models. In B. Schölkopf, J. Platt, and T. Hoffman, editors, *Advances in Neural Information Processing Systems 19*, pages 641–648. MIT Press, Cambridge, MA.

Dan Klein and Chris Manning. 2004. Corpus-based induction of syntactic structure: Models of dependency and constituency. In *Proceedings of the 42nd Annual Meeting of the Association for Computational Linguistics*, pages 478–485.

Roger Levy. 2008. Expectation-based syntactic comprehension. *Cognition*, 106:1126–1177.

John W. Lloyd. 1987. *Foundations of Logic Programming*. Springer, Berlin, 2 edition.

David M. Magerman. 1995. Statistical decision-tree models for parsing. In *The Proceedings of the 33rd Annual Meeting of the Association for Computational Linguistics*, pages 276–283, San Francisco. The Association for Computational Linguistics, Morgan Kaufman.

Michell P. Marcus, Beatrice Santorini, and Mary Ann Marcinkiewicz. 1993. Building a large annotated corpus of English: The Penn Treebank. *Computational Linguistics*, 19(2):313–330.

David Marr. 1982. *Vision*. W.H. Freeman and Company, New York.

Matha Palmer, Daniel Gildea, and Paul Kingsbury. 2005. The Proposition Bank: An annotated corpus of semantic roles. *Computational Linguistics*, 31(1):71–106.

Joe Pater. 2008. Gradual learning and convergence. *Linguistic Inquiry*, 30(2):334–345.

Judea Pearl. 1988. *Probabalistic Reasoning in Intelligent Systems: Networks of Plausible Inference*. Morgan Kaufmann, San Mateo, California.

Slav Petrov and Dan Klein. 2007. Improved inference for unlexicalized parsing. In *Human Language Technologies 2007: The Conference of the North American Chapter of the Association for Computational Linguistics; Proceedings of the Main Conference*, pages 404–411, Rochester, New York, April. Association for Computational Linguistics.

Geoffrey K. Pullum. 2007. Ungrammaticality, rarity, and corpus use. *Corpus Linguistics and Linguistic Theory*, 3:33–47.

Brian Roark. 2001. Probabilistic top-down parsing and language modeling. *Computational Linguistics*, 27(2):249–276.

Stuart M. Shieber. 1986. *An Introduction to Unification-based Approaches to Grammar*. CSLI Lecture Notes Series. Chicago University Press, Chicago.

Paul Smolensky and Géraldine Legendre. 2005. *The Harmonic Mind: From Neural Computation To Optimality-Theoretic Grammar*. The MIT Press.

Computational Linguistics and Generative Linguistics: The Triumph of Hope over Experience

Geoffrey K. Pullum
School of Philosophy, Psychology, and Language Sciences
University of Edinburgh
gpullum@ling.ed.ac.ul

Abstract

It is remarkable if any relationship at all persists between computational linguists (CL) and that part of general linguistics comprising the mainstream of MIT transformational-generative (TG) theoretical syntax. If the lines are still open, it represents something of a tribute to CL practitioners' tolerance — a triumph of hope and goodwill over the experience of abuse — because the TG community has shown considerable hostility toward CL and everything it stands for over the past fifty years. I offer some brief historical notes, and hint at prospects for a better basis for collaboration in the future.

1 Introduction

The theme of this workshop is the interaction between computational linguistics (CL) and general linguistics. The organizers ask whether it has it been virtuous, vicious, or vacuous. They use only three of the rather extraordinary number of *v*-initial adjectives. Is the relationship vital, valuable, venturesome, visionary, versatile, and vibrant? Or vague, variable, verbose, and sometimes vexatious? Has it perhaps been merely vestigial and vicarious, with hardly any general linguists really participating? Or vain, venal, vaporous, virginal, volatile, and voguish, yet vulnerable, a relationship at risk? Or would the best description use adjectives like vengeful, venomous, vilificatory, villainous, vindictive, violent, vitriolic, vociferous, and vulpine?

I will argue that at least with respect to that part of general linguistics comprising the mainstream of American theoretical syntax, it would be quite remarkable if any relationship with computational linguistics (CL) had thrived. It would represent (as Samuel Johnson remarked cynically, and wrongly, about second marriages) a triumph of hope over experience. It seems to me that the relationship that could have been was at least somewhat blighted by the negative and defensive stance that MIT-influenced transformational-generative (TG) syntacticians have adopted on a diverse array of topics highly relevant to CL.

There was never any need for such attitudes. And at the conclusion of these brief remarks I will suggest a basis for thinking that relations could be much more satisfactory in the future. But I think it is worth taking a sober look at the half-century of history from 1959 to 2009, during which almost everything about the course of theoretical syntax, at least in the USA, where I worked during the latter half of the period, has been tacitly guided by a single line of thinking. 'Generative grammar' is commonly used to denote it, but that will not do. First, 'generative grammar' is often used to mean 'MIT-influenced transformational-generative grammar'. For that I will use the abbreviation TG. And second, it is sometimes (incorrectly) claimed that 'generative' means nothing more or less than 'explicit' (see Chomsky 1966, 12: 'a *generative grammar* (that is, an explicit grammar that makes no appeal to the reader's "faculé de langage" but rather attempts to incorporate the mechanisms of this faculty)').

We need more precise terminology in order to home in on what I am talking about. As Seuren (2004) has stressed, the relevant vision of what a grammar is like, built into most linguistic theorization today at a level so deep that most linguists are incapable of seeing past it or out of it, is not just that it is explicit, but that a grammar is and must be a syntax-centered random generator. I will therefore refer to **language specification by random generation** (LSRG).

The definitive technical paper defining grammars in LSRG terms is Chomsky (1959). This was a fine paper, which would have earned its

Proceedings of the EACL 2009 Workshop on the Interaction between Linguistics and Computational Linguistics, pages 12–21, Athens, Greece, 30 March, 2009.

writer tenure in any department of linguistics, logic, computer science, or mathematics that knew what it was doing and could see the possibilities. But it brought into linguistics two things that were not going to go away for half a century. One was the notion that any formally precise linguistics had to be limited to LSRG. And the other was the combative and insular personality of the paper's author, which had such a great influence on the personality of his extraordinarily important department at MIT.

2 Obsession with random generation

The sense of 'generate' relevant to LSRG goes back to the work of the great mathematical logician Emil Post (as acknowledged by Chomsky 1959, 137n). Post's project was initially to formalize the notion of proof in logical systems — originally, the propositional logic that was informally used but not formally defined in Whitehead and Russell's *Principia Mathematica*. He represented well-formed formulae ('enunciations', including the 'primitive assertions', i.e. axioms, and the 'assertions' i.e. theorems) to be simply strings over a finite set of symbols, and rules of inference ('productions') as instructions for deriving a new string (the conclusion) from a set of strings already in hand (the premises). He then studied the question of what kinds of sets of strings could be generated if a set of initial strings were closed under the operation of applying inference rules. Post's rather ungainly general presentation of the general concept of rules of inference, or in his terms **productions**, looks like this:

$$
\begin{array}{c}
g_{1_1}\, P_{i'_1}\, g_{1_2}\, P_{i'_2}\, \cdots\, g_{1_{m_1}}\, P_{i'_{m_1}}\, g_{1_{m_1+1}} \\
g_{2_1}\, P_{i''_1}\, g_{2_2}\, P_{i''_2}\, \cdots\, g_{2_{m_2}}\, P_{i''_{m_2}}\, g_{2_{m_2+1}} \\
\cdots\cdots\cdots\cdots \\
g_{k_1}\, P_{i'^k_1}\, g_{k_2}\, P_{i'^k_2}\, \cdots\, g_{k_{m_k}}\, P_{i'^k_{m_k}}\, g_{k_{m_k+1}} \\
\text{produce} \\
g_1\, P_{i_1}\, g_2\, P_{i_2}\, \cdots\, g_m\, P_{i_m}\, g_{m+1}
\end{array}
$$

In specific instances of productions the g metavariables in this schema are replaced by actual strings over what is now known as the **terminal vocabulary**. The P metavariables function as cover symbols for arbitrary stretches of material — they are string variables, some of which may be repeated to copy material into the conclusion. A production provides a license, given a set of strings that match patterns of the form $g_0P_1g_1P_2 \cdots P_kg_k$, to produce a certain other string composed in some way out of the various g_i and P_i.

Post defined a class of **canonical systems**, each consisting of a set of initial strings and a finite set of productions. Sets generated by canonical production systems he called **canonical sets**. Post had realized early on that the canonical sets were nothing more or less than the sets definable by recursive functions or Turing machines; that is, they were just the recursively enumerable (r. e.) sets.

He proceeded to prove that even if you restrict the number and distribution of the g_i and P_i extremely tightly, expressive power may not be reduced. Specifically, he proved that no reduction in the definable sets is obtained even if you set the number of P variables and the number of premises at 1, and require that every production has the form 'g_0P produces Pg_1'. Such very restricted systems were called **normal systems**. Normal systems can still derive every canonical set, provided you are allowed to use extra symbols that appear in derivations but not in the ultimately generated strings (these extra symbols are what would become known to formal language theorists within computer science as **variables** and to linguists as **nonterminals**).

In a notation more familiar to linguists, the result amounts to showing that every r. e. subset of Σ^+ can be generated by some generative grammar using a symbol vocabulary $V = \Sigma \cup N$ in which all rules have the form '$xW \rightarrow Wy$' for specified strings $x, y \in V^*$ and some fixed $W \in V^*$. This was the first weak generative capacity result: normal systems are equivalent in weak generative capacity to full canonical systems.

In a later paper, settling a conjecture of Thue, Post showed (1947) that you can derive every canonical set if your productions all have the form '$P_1g_iP_2$ produces $P_1g_jP_2$'. This amounts to showing that every canonical subset of Σ^+ can be generated by (what would later be called) a generative grammar using a symbol vocabulary $V = \Sigma \cup N$ in which all rules have the form '$WxZ \rightarrow WyZ$' for specified strings $x, y \in V^*$ and fixed $W, Z \in V^*$.

Hence the first demonstration that unrestricted rewriting systems (Chomsky's 'type-0' grammars) can derive any r. e. set was not original with Chomsky (1959). It had been published twelve years earlier by Post.

Post had in effect invented what could be called

top-down random generators. These randomly generate r. e. sets of symbols by expanding an initial axiomatic string, which can be just a single symbol. Their equivalence to Turing machines is obvious (Kozen 1997, 256–257).

Between the time of Post's doctoral work in 1920 and the 1943 paper in which he published his result on canonical systems (already present in compressed form in his thesis), Ajdukiewicz (1935) had proposed a different style of generative grammar, also motivated by the development of a better understanding of proof. Adjukiewicz's invention was categorial grammar, the first kind of **bottom-up random generators**. It composes expressions of the generated language by combining parts — initially primitive categorized symbols, and then previously composed subparts.

When Chomsky and Lasnik (1977) start talking about the 'computational system' of human language (a mode of speaking that rapidly caught on, and persists in current 'minimalist' work), the 'computation' of which they spoke was one that takes place nowhere: no such computations are ever done, except perhaps using pencil and paper as a syntactic theorist tries to figure out how or whether a certain string can be derived. This 'computational system' attempts randomly and nondeterministically to find some way to apply rules in order to build a particular structure, starting from an arbitrary syntactic starting point.

In the case of pre-1990 work the starting point was apparently a start symbol; in post-1990 'minimalist' work it is a **numeration**: a randomly chosen multiset of categorized items from the lexicon. The concept of a 'numeration' is a reflection of how firmly embedded the random-generation idea is. The numeration serves no real purpose. It would be possible to formalize a grammar as a set of combinatory principles for putting together words in a string as encountered, from first to last, so that it was in effect a parser. Categorial grammars seem ideally suited to that role (Steedman, 2000), and minimalist grammars are really just a variety of categorial grammar, stripped of some of the formal coherence and links to logic and semantics.

Chomsky has often written as if it were a necessary truth that a grammar must be a random generator. For example: 'Clearly, a grammar must contain ... a 'syntactic component' that generates an infinite number of strings representing grammatical sentences ... This is the classical model for grammar' (Chomsky 1962, 539). This says that a grammar *must* be a random generator. But this is not true. A grammar could in principle be formulated as, say a transducer mapping phonetic representation inputs to corresponding sets of logical forms. (Presumably this must be possible, given what human beings do.)

It is particularly strange to see Chomsky ignoring this possibility and yet asserting in *Knowledge of Language* (Chomsky, 1986b) that a person's internalized grammar 'assigns a status to every relevant physical event, say, every sound wave' (p. 26). The claim is false, simply because random generators are not transducers or functions: they do not take inputs. A random generator only 'assigns a status' to a string by generating it with a derivation that associates it with certain properties. And surely it is not a sensible hypothesis about human linguistic competence to posit that in the brain of every human being there is an internalized random generator generating every physically possible sequence of sounds, from a ship's foghorn to Mahler's ninth symphony.

3 Downplaying expressive power

Perhaps the most centrally important reason for linguists' concern with the possibility of excess expressive power in grammar formalisms was their sense that it should be guaranteed by the general theory of grammar that linguistic behaviors such as understanding a sentence should be represented as at least possible. This meant that grammars had to be defined in a way that at least made the general membership problem ('Given grammar G, is string w grammatical?') decidable.

It was in Chomsky's 1959 paper that progress was first made toward restricting the expressive power of production systems in ways that achieved this, and the early work on topics like pushdown automata and finite state machines shows that those topics were of interest.

As is well known, Chomsky showed that if productions of the general form $X\varphi Z \rightarrow X\psi Z$ (where X, ψ, Z are strings in V^* and $\varphi \in V^+$) are limited by the condition that ψ is no shorter than φ, we are no longer able to derive every r. e. set of strings over the alphabet; we get only the context-sensitive stringsets. If the further limitation that $\varphi \in N$ is imposed, we get only the context-free stringsets. And if on top of that the requirement that $\psi \in (\Sigma \cup \Sigma N)$ is imposed, we get only the regular sets.

Chomsky's 1959 position was that the set of all grammatical English word sequences was not a regular stringset over the set of English words, and that if any context-free grammar for English could be constructed, it would not be an elegant or revealing one. The search for intuitively adequate grammars therefore had to range over the class of grammars generating context-sensitive stringsets. This is a large class of grammars, but at least it is a proper subset of the class of grammars for which the membership recognition problem is decidable. Casting around outside that range was probably not sensible, since natural languages surely had to be decidable (it was taken to be quite obvious that native speakers could rapidly recognize whether or not a string of words was a sentence in their language).

As I have detailed elsewhere in somewhat tongue-in-cheek fashion (Pullum, 1989), Chomsky pulled back sharply from his initial interest in mathematical study of linguistic formalisms as it became clear that TG theories were being criticized for their Turing-equivalence, and began dismissing precise studies of the generative capacity of grammars as trivial and ridiculous. This, it seems to me, was one more clear sign of distancing from the concerns of CL. It was mainly computational linguists who showed interest in Gazdar's observation that a theory limited to generating context-free languages could guarantee not just recognition but recognition in polynomial (indeed, better than cubic) time, and in the related observation that none of the arguments for non-context-free characteristics in human languages seemed to be good ones (Pullum and Gazdar, 1982).

The MIT reaction to Gazdar's suggestion was to mount a major effort to find intractability in Gazdar-style (GPSG) grammars — to represent the recognition problem as NP-hard even for context-free-equivalent theories of grammar (Barton et al., 1987). This was something of a confidence trick. First, the results depended on switching attention from the fixed-grammar arbitrary-string recognition problem (the analog of what Vardi (1982) calls data complexity) to the variable-grammar arbitrary-string recognition problem (what Vardi calls combined complexity). Second, it seemed to be vaguely assumed that only GPSG had any charges to answer, and that the GB theory of that time (Chomsky, 1981) would not suffer from similar computational complexity problems, but GB eventually turned out to be, insofar as it was well defined, strongly equivalent to Gazdar's framework (Rogers, 1998).

For pre-GB varieties of TG, however, the problem had mainly been not that recognition was NP-hard but that it was not computable at all: transformational grammars from 1957 on kept proving to be Turing-equivalent. That was what seems to have driven the denigration of mathematical linguistics, and the downplaying of the relevance of decidability to such an extreme degree (see e.g. Chomsky 1980: 120ff, where the very idea that recognition is decidable is dismissed as an unimportant detail, and not necessarily even a true claim).

4 Hostility to machine testing

With many versions of TG offering no guarantee that there was any parser for the language even in principle, it was not clear that machine testing of grammatical theories by algorithmic checking of claims made about grammaticality of selected strings was a plausible idea. Perhaps machine theorem-proving algorithms could have been adapted to showing that a certain grammar could indeed derive a certain string, but in practice early transformational grammar was vastly too complex to permit the building of tools for grammar testing, and later transformational grammar far too vague.

I know of only one success story in grammar evaluation by implementing random generation, in fact. Ed Stabler (1992) coded up a Prolog grammaticality-proving system based on the *Barriers* theory of transformational grammar (Chomsky, 1986a), which (Pullum, 1989) had mocked for sloppiness of statement. The *Barriers* system had in particular abandoned the usual practice of defining trees in a way that had dominance as a reflexive relation. Chomsky casually asserted that he would take it to be irreflexive. Moreover, Stabler's careful and sympathetic reconstruction of Chomsky's intent defines the notion of 'exclusion' in such a way that every node excludes itself (Chomsky's definition said that 'α excludes β if [and only if] no segment of α dominates β', and of course a given α never dominates itself). And sure enough, the Stabler implementation revealed that this system of definitions had a problem: unbounded dependency constructions that Chomsky took to be allowed were in fact blocked by his theoretical machinery.

Stabler concluded from his discovery 'that the project of implementing GB theories transparently is both manageable and worthwhile'. But his paper has essentially never been referred to by any mainstream syntacticians. It was not exactly what they wanted to hear. Nor has anyone, to my knowledge, utilized Stabler's experience in doing syntactic research using the *Barriers* framework.

There has in any case traditionally been considerable resistance to machine testing of theories. I have heard a story told by MIT linguists of how one early graduate student devised a computer program to test the rule system of SPE, and told Morris Halle about some of the bugs he had thereby found, but Halle had already noticed all of them. The moral of the story is clearly supposed to be that machine testing is unneeded and of no value.

Mark Johnson as an undergraduate did some work showing that the Unix stream editor **sed** could serve as an excellent tool for implementing systems of ordered historical sound changes for the assistance of comparative-historical linguists; but this very sensible idea never led to widespread testing of synchronic phonological ordered-rule analyses.

In short, computational testbeds, however enthusiastically developed in some areas of science (chemistry, astrophysics, ecology, molecular biology), simply never (yet) took off in linguistic science.

5 Loathing of corpora

There has traditionally been hostility even to machine data-hunting or language study through computer-searchable corpora. This is fading away as a new generation of young linguists who do everything by searching the web do their data by web search too; but it held back collaboration for a long time. Early proposals for amassing computer corpora were treated with contempt by TG grammarians ('I'm a native speaker, I have intuitions; why do I need your arbitrary collection of computer-searchable text?').

And quite often evidence from attested sentences is simply dismissed. To take a random example, on page 48 of Postal (1971) the sentences *I am annoying to myself* is prefixed with an asterisk to show that it is ungrammatical. Searching for this exact strings using Google, as we can do today, reveals that it gets 229 hits. I take this multiple attestation to shift the burden overwhelmingly against the linguist who claims that it is barred by the grammar of the language. But anyone who has experience (as I do) with trying to talk TG linguists out of their beliefs by citing attested sentences will know that it is between the difficult and the impossible. From 'There are many errors in published works' to 'It may be OK for him, but it's not for me', there are many ways in which the linguist can escape from the conclusion that a machine has proved superior in assessing the data.

Hostility to corpus work has probably to some extent paved the way for the present situation, where the machine translation teams at Google's research labs has no linguists, the work depending entirely on heavily numerical tracking of statistical parallels seen in aligned bilingual texts.

And an unwholesome split is visible in the linguistics community between those who broadly want nothing to do with corpora and think personal intuitions are fine as a basis for data gathering, and the people that I have called corpus fetishists who treat all facts as unclean and unholy unless they come direct and unedited out of a corpus. At the extremes, we get a divide between dreamers and token-counters — on the one hand, people who think that speculations on how universal principles might account for subtle shades of their own inner reactions to particular sentences, and on the other, people who think that counting the different pronouns in ten million words of text and tabulating the results is a contribution to science.

6 Aversion to the stochastic

Mention of statistics reminds us that stochastic methods have revolutionized CL since the 1980s, but have made few inroads into general linguistics, and none into TG linguistics. This is despite the excellent introduction to probabilistic generative grammars provided in Levelt's excellent and far-sighted introduction to mathematical linguistics (Levelt, 1974), the first volume of which has now been republished separately (Levelt, 2008).

The reason for the extraordinarily low profile of probabilistic grammars within the ranks of TG linguists has to do with the very successful attack on the very possibility of their relevance in *Syntac-*

tic Structures (Chomsky, 1957). Insisting that any statistical model for grammaticality would have to treat *Colorless green ideas sleep furiously* and *Furiously sleep ideas green colorless* in exactly the same terms, as they are word strings with the same (pre-1957) frequency of zero, Chomsky argued that probability of a string had no conceivable relevance to its grammaticality.

Unfortunately he had made a mistake. He was tacitly assuming that the probability of an event type that has not yet occurred must be zero. Maximum likelihood estimation (MLE) does indeed yield that result; but Chomsky was not obliged to adopt MLE. The technique now known as smoothing had been developed during the Second World War by Alan Turing and I. J. Good, and although it took a while to become known, Good had published on it by 1953. Chomsky was simply not acquainted with the statistical literature and not interested in applying statistical methods to linguistic material. Most linguists for the next forty years followed him in his disdain for such work. But when Pereira (2000) finally applied Good-Turing estimation (smoothing) to the question of how different the probabilities of the two famous word sequences are from normal English text, he found that the first (the syntactically well-formed one) had a probability 200,000 times that of the second.

7 Contempt for applications

Theoretical linguists have tended to have an almost total lack of interest in anything that might offer a practical application for their theories. Most kinds of science tend eventually to support some sort of engineering or practical techniques: physics led to jet planes; geology gave us oil location methods; biology brought forth gene splicing; even logic and psychology have applications in factories and other workplaces. But not mainstream theoretical linguistics. Its theories do not seem to yield applications of any sort.

Very early on, Chomsky found that he had to distance himself from computers altogether: note the remark in Chomsky (1966, 9) that 'Quite a few commentators have assumed that recent work in generative grammar is somehow an outgrowth of an interest in the use of computers for one or another purpose, or that it has some engineering motivation', and note that he calls such views both 'incomprehensible' and 'entirely false'. Being taken to have ambitions relating to natural language processing was at that time clearly anathema for the leader of the TG community.

What takes the place of application of theories to practical domains today, since nothing has come of any computational TG linguistics, is an attempt to derive conclusions about human brain organization and mental anatomy. Linguists claim to be biologists rather than psychologists (psycholinguistics developed its own experimental paradigms and began its own steady progress away from interaction with TG linguistics). There is a journal called *Biolinguistics* now, and much talk about interfaces and evolution and perfection. Linguists somehow live with the fact that the real biologists and neurophysiologists are not getting involved.

It is probably this pretense at uncovering deep principles of structure in a putative mental organ (and pretense is what it is) that is responsible for the dramatic falling off of interest in precise description of languages. Getting the details right — what was described as 'observational adequacy' in *Aspects* (Chomsky, 1965) — is taken to be a low-prestige occupation when compared to one that is alleged to offer glimpses of universal principles that hold the key to language acquisition and the innate cognitive abilities of the species.

Yet these universal principles are never actually presented for examination in the way that genuine results in science are. It is as if what is important to the hunter after universal principles is the hunt itself, the call of the horn and the thrill of the chase, but not the grubby business of examining and weighing the kill. The fact is that no really robust and carefully formulated universals of language have been discovered, described, promulgated, confirmed, and widely accepted as correct in the fifty years that universals have been sought.

The notion that linguists have discovered innate principles that solve the mystery of first language acquisition (Scholz and Pullum, 2006) is particularly pernicious. The position generally advocated by TG linguists is widely known as **linguistic nativism**, and it says that some significant aspects of knowledge of language are not derived from any experience but are innately known. But when pressed on the question of what the evidence shows about linguistic nativism, about whether it can really be defended against its plausible rivals, nativists tend to react by drawing back very sharply into a trivial form of the thesis: of course linguistic nativism must be true, they insist, because when you raise a baby and a kitten in the same household under the same conditions it is only the baby ends up with knowledge of language. They therefore differ in some respect, innately. 'Universal grammar' is simply one name that linguists use for that which separates them: whatever it is that human infants have but kittens and monkeys and bricks don't.

But of course, that makes the thesis trivial: it is true in virtue of being merely a restatement of the observation that led to linguistic nativism being put forward. We know that it is only human neonates who accomplish the language acquisition task, and that is why we are seeking an explanatory theory of how humans accomplish the task. To say that there must be something special about them is certainly true, but that does not count as a scientific discovery. We need specifics. Serious scientists are like the private sector as characterized in the immortal line uttered by Ray Stantz (played by Dan Ackroyd) in *Ghostsbusters*: 'I've worked in the private sector. They expect results!'

8 Hope for the future

It is absolutely not the case that general and theoretical linguistics should continue to act as if the main object were to prevent any interaction with CL. Let me point to a few hopeful developments.

Over the period from about 1989 to 2001, a team of linguists worked on and completed a truly comprehensive informal grammar of the English language. It was published as Huddleston and Pullum et al. (2002), henceforth *CGEL*. It is an informal grammar, intended for serious academic users but not limited to those with a linguistics background. And it comes close to being fully exhaustive in its coverage of Standard English grammatical constructions and morphology.

It should not be forgotten that the era of TG, though it produced (in my view) no theories that are really worth having, an enormous number of interesting data discoveries about English were made. *CGEL* profited greatly from those, as the Further Reading section makes clear. But does not attempt to develop theoretical conclusions or participate in theoretical disputes. Wherever possible, *CGEL* takes a largely pretheoretic or at least basically neutral stance.

Where theoretical commitments have to be made explicit, they are, but they are then implemented in consistent terms across the entire book. Although more than a dozen linguists were involved, it is not an anthology; Huddleston and Pullum provide a unitary authorial voice for the book and rewrote every part of the book at least once. When disputes about analyses arose between the authors who drafted different chapters, they were settled one way or the other by recourse to evidence, and not permitted to create departures from consistency in the book as a whole.

CGEL was preceded by large-scale 3-volume grammars for Italian (Renzi et al., 2001) and for Spanish (Bosque and Demonte, 1999), and now a grammar of French on a similar scale, the *Grande Grammaire du français* is being written by a team of linguists in Paris under the leadership of Anne Abeillé (Paris 7), Annie Delaveau (Paris 10), and Danièle Godard (CNRS). In 2006 I visited Paris at the request of that team to give a workshop on the making of *CGEL*. Work continues, and the book is now planned for publication by Editions Bayard in 2010. If anything the scope of this work is broader than *CGEL*'s, since *CGEL* did not aim to cover uncontroversially non-standard dialects of English (for example, those that have negative concord), whereas the *Grande Grammaire* explicitly aims to cover regional and non-standard varieties of French. Additionally, an effort to produce a comparable grammar of Mandarin Chinese is now being mounted in Hong Kong under the directorship of Professor Chu-Ren Huang, the dean of the new Faculty of Humanities at Hong Kong Polytechnic University. I gave a workshop on *CGEL* there (in March 2009) too.

The importance of these projects is simply that they bear witness to the fact that, at least in some areas, there are linguists — and not just isolated individuals but teams of experienced linguists — who are prepared to get involved in detailed language description of the type that will be a prerequisite to any future computational linguistics that relies on details of syntax and semantics (rather than probabilistic number-crunching on n-grams and raw text, which has its own interest but does not involve input from linguistics or even a rudimentary knowledge of the language being processed). Among them are both traditional general linguists like Huddleston and people with serious CL experience like Abeillé and Huang.

But there is more. I have made a preliminary analysis of the inventory of syntactic categories used in the tagging for labelling trees in the

Penn Treebank (Marcus et al., 1993), comparing them to the categories used in *CGEL*. I would describe the fit as not perfect, but within negotiating range. In some ways the fit is remarkable, given the complete independence of the two projects (the Treebank under Mitch Marcus in Philadelphia was largely complete by 1992, when the *CGEL* project under the direction of Rodney Huddleston in Australia was only just getting up to speed, but Huddleston and Marcus did not know about each other's work).

The biggest discrepancy in categorization is in the problematic area of prepositions, adverbs, and subordinating conjunctions, where the Treebank has remained much too close to the confused older tradition (where many prepositions are claimed to have second lives as adverbs and quite a few are also included on the list of subordinating conjunctions, so that a word like *since* has one meaning but three grammatical categories). The heart of the problem is that the sage counsel of Jespersen (1924, 87–90) and the cogent arguments of Emonds (1972) were not taken under consideration by the devisers of the Treebank's tagging categories. But fixing that would involve nothing more than undoing some unmotivated partitioning of the preposition category.

Since there are few if any significant disagreements about bracketing, and the category systems could be brought into alignment, I believe it would not be a major project to convert the entire Penn Treebank into an alternate form where it was totally compatible with *CGEL* in the syntactic analyses it presupposed. There could be considerable value in a complex of reference tools that included a treebank of some 4.5 million words that is fully compatible in its syntactic assumptions with an 1,860-page reference grammar of high reliability and consistency.

And there is yet more. Here I will be brief, and things will get slightly technical. The question naturally arises of how one might formalize *CGEL* to get it in a form where it was explicit enough for use as a database that natural language processing systems could in principle make use of. James Rogers and I have recently considered that question (Pullum and Rogers, 2008) within the context of model-theoretic syntax, a line of work that first began to receive sophisticated formulations here at the EACL in various papers of the early 1990s (e.g. Blackburn et al. (1993), Kracht (1993), Blackburn & Gardent (1995); see Pullum (2007) for a brief historical survey, and Pullum & Scholz (2001) for a deeper treatment of relevant theoretical issues).

One thing that might appear to be a stumbling-block to formalizing *CGEL*, and an obstacle to the relationship with treebanks as well, is that strictly speaking *CGEL*'s assumed syntactic representations are not (or not all) trees. They are graphs that depart from being ordinary constituent-structure trees in at least two respects.

First, they are annotated not just with categories labelling the nodes, but also with syntactic functions (grammatical relations like Subject-of, Determiner-of, Head-of, Complement-of, etc.) that are perhaps best conceptualized as labelling the edges of the graph (the lines between the nodes in the diagrams).

Second, and perhaps more seriously, there is occasional downward convergence of branches: it is permitted for a given constituent, under certain conditions, to bear two different grammatical relations to two different superordinate nodes. (A determinative like *some*, for example, may be both the Determiner of an NP and the Head of the Nominal that is the phrasal head of that NP.) Often (as in HPSG work) the introduction of re-entrancy had dramatic consequences for key properties like decidability of satisfiability for descriptions, or even for model-checking. (I take it that the formal issues around HPSG are very well known to the EACL community. In this short paper I do not try to deal with HPSG at all. There is plenty to be said, but also plenty of excellent HPSG specialists in Europe who are more competent than I am to treat the topic.)

Pullum & Rogers (2008) shows, however, that given certain very weak conditions, which seem almost certainly to be satisfied by the kinds of grammatical analysis posited in grammars of the *CGEL* sort, there is a way of constructing a compatible directed ordered spanning tree for any *CGEL*-style syntactic structure in such a way that no information is lost and reachability via edge chains is preserved. Moreover, the mapping between *CGEL* structures and spanning trees is definable in weak monadic second-order logic (wMSO).

Put this together with the results of Rogers (1998) on definability of trees in wMSO, and there is a clear prospect of the *CGEL* analysis of English syntax being reconstructible in terms of the wMSO theory of trees. And what that means for parsing is clear from results of nearly 40 years ago (Doner, 1970): there is a strong equivalence via tree automata to context-free grammars, which means that all the technology of context-free parsing can potentially be brought to bear on processing them.

This does not mean it would be a crisis if some language of interest is found to be non-context-free, incidentally. By the results of Rogers (2003), wMSO theories interpreted on tree-like structures of higher dimensionality than 2 could be employed. For example, where the structures are 3-dimensional (so that individual nodes are allowed to bear the parent-of relation to all of the nodes in entire 2-dimensional trees), the string yield of the set of all structures satisfying a given wMSO sentence is always a tree-adjoining language, and for every tree-adjoining language there is such a characterizing wMSO sentence.

Notice, by the way, that the theoretical tools of use here are coming out of currently very active subdisciplines of computational logic and automata theory, such as finite model theory, descriptive complexity theory, and database theory. The very tools that linguistics needs in order to formalize syntactic theories in a revealing way are the ones that theoretical computer science is intensively working on because their investigation is intrinsically interesting.

To sum up, what this is all telling us is that there is no reason for anyone to continue being guided by the TG bias toward isolating theoretical linguistics from CL. There is not necessarily a major gulf between (i) cutting-edge current theoretical developments like model-theoretic syntax, (ii) large-scale descriptive grammars like *CGEL*, and (iii) feasible computational natural-language engineering. Given the excellent personal relations between general linguists and computational linguists in some European locations (Edinburgh being an excellent example), it seems to me that developments in interdisciplinary relations that would integrate the two disciplines quite thoroughly could probably happen quite fast. Perhaps it is happening already.

Acknowledgments

I am very grateful to Barbara Scholz for her detailed criticisms of a draft of this paper. I have taken account of many of her helpful suggestions, but since she still does not agree with what I say here, none of the failings or errors above should be blamed on her.

References

Kazimierz Ajdukiewicz. 1935. Die syntaktische konnexität. *Studia Philosophica*, 1:1–27. Reprinted in Storrs McCall, ed., *Polish Logic 1920–1939*, 207–231. Oxford: Oxford University Press.

G. Edward Barton, Robert C. Berwick, and Eric Sven Ristad. 1987. *Computational Complexity and Natural Language*. MIT Press, Cambridge, MA.

Patrick Blackburn and Claire Gardent. 1995. A specification language for lexical functional grammars. In *Seventh Conference of the European Chapter of the Association for Computational Linguistics: Proceedings of the Conference*, pages 39–44, Morristown, NJ. European Association for Computational Linguistics.

Patrick Blackburn, Claire Gardent, and Wilfried Meyer-Viol. 1993. Talking about trees. In *Sixth Conference of the European Chapter of the Association for Computational Linguistics: Proceedings of the Conference*, pages 21–29, Morristown, NJ. European Association for Computational Linguistics.

Ignacio Bosque and Violeta Demonte, editors. 1999. *Gramática Descriptiva de La Lengua Española*. Real Academia Española / Espasa Calpe, Madrid. 3 volumes.

Noam Chomsky and Howard Lasnik. 1977. Filters and control. *Linguistic Inquiry*, 8:425–504.

Noam Chomsky. 1957. *Syntactic Structures*. Mouton, The Hague.

Noam Chomsky. 1959. On certain formal properties of grammars. *Information and Control*, 2:137–167. Reprinted in *Readings in Mathematical Psychology*, Volume II, ed. by R. Duncan Luce, Robert R. Bush, and Eugene Galanter, 125–155, New York: John Wiley & Sons, 1965 (citation to the original on p. 125 of this reprinting is incorrect).

Noam Chomsky. 1962. Explanatory models in linguistics. In Ernest Nagel, Patrick Suppes, and Alfred Tarski, editors, *Logic, Methodology and Philosophy of Science: Proceedings of the 1960 International Congress*, pages 528–550, Stanford, CA. Stanford University Press.

Noam Chomsky. 1965. *Aspects of the Theory of Syntax*. MIT Press, Cambridge, MA.

Noam Chomsky. 1966. *Topics in the Theory of Generative Grammar*. Mouton, The Hague.

Noam Chomsky. 1980. *Rules and Representations*. Basil Blackwell, Oxford.

Noam Chomsky. 1981. *Lectures on Government and Binding*. Foris, Dordrecht.

Noam Chomsky. 1986a. *Barriers*. MIT Press, Cambridge, MA.

Noam Chomsky. 1986b. *Knowledge of Language: Its Origins, Nature, and Use*. Praeger, New York.

John Doner. 1970. Tree acceptors and some of their applications. *Journal of Computer and System Sciences*, 4:406–451.

Joseph E. Emonds. 1972. Evidence that indirect object movement is a structure-preserving rule. *Foundations of Language*, 8:546–561.

Rodney Huddleston, Geoffrey K. Pullum, et al. 2002. *The Cambridge Grammar of the English Language*. Cambridge University Press, Cambridge.

Otto Jespersen. 1924. *The Philosophy of Grammar*. Holt, New York.

Dexter Kozen. 1997. *Automata and Computability*. Springer, Berlin.

Marcus Kracht. 1993. Mathematical aspects of command relations. In *Sixth Conference of the European Chapter of the Association for Computational Linguistics: Proceedings of the Conference*, pages 240–249, Morristown, NJ. Association for Computational Linguistics.

W. J. M. Levelt. 1974. *Formal Grammars in Linguistics and Psycholinguistics. Volume I: An Introduction to the Theory of Formal Languages and Automata; Volume II: Applications in Linguistic Theory; Volume III: Psycholinguistic Applications*. Mouton, The Hague.

W. J. M. Levelt. 2008. *An Introduction to the Theory of Formal Languages and Automata*. John Benjamins, Amsterdam.

Mitchell Marcus, Beatrice Santorini, and Mary Ann Marcinkiewicz. 1993. Building a large annotated corpus of English: the Penn Treebank. *Computational Linguistics*, 19(2):313–330.

Emil Post. 1947. Recursive unsolvability of a problem of thue. *Journal of Symbolic Logic*, 12:1–11.

Paul M. Postal. 1971. *Crossover Phenomena*. Holt, Rinehart and Winston, New York.

Geoffrey K. Pullum and Gerald Gazdar. 1982. Natural languages and context-free languages. *Linguistics and Philosophy*, 4:471–504.

Geoffrey K. Pullum and James Rogers. 2008. Expressive power of the syntactic theory implicit in *the cambridge grammar of the english language*. Paper presented at the annual meeting of the Linguistics Association of Great Britain, University of Essex, September 2008. Online at http://ling.ed.ac.uk/~gpullum/EssexLAGB.pdf.

Geoffrey K. Pullum and Barbara C. Scholz. 2001. On the distinction between model-theoretic and generative-enumerative syntactic frameworks. In Philippe de Groote, Glyn Morrill, and Christian Retoré, editors, *Logical Aspects of Computational Linguistics: 4th International Conference*, number 2099 in Lecture Notes in Artificial Intelligence, pages 17–43, Berlin and New York. Springer.

Geoffrey K. Pullum. 1989. Formal linguistics meets the Boojum. *Natural Language & Linguistic Theory*, 7:137–143.

Geoffrey K. Pullum. 2007. The evolution of model-theoretic frameworks in linguistics. In James Rogers and Stephan Kepser, editors, *Model-Theoretic Syntax at 10: ESSLLI 2007 Workshop*, pages 1–10, Trinity College Dublin, Ireland. Association for Logic, Language and Information.

Lorenzo Renzi, Giampaolo Salvi, and Anna Cardinaletti. 2001. *Grande grammatica italiana di consultazione*. Il Mulino, Bologna. 3 volumes.

James Rogers. 1998. *A Descriptive Approach to Language-Theoretic Complexity*. CSLI Publications, Stanford, CA.

James Rogers. 2003. wMSO theories as grammar formalisms. *Theoretical Computer Science*, 293:291–320.

Barbara C. Scholz and Geoffrey K. Pullum. 2006. Irrational nativist exuberance. In Robert Stainton, editor, *Contemporary Debates in Cognitive Science*, pages 59–80. Basil Blackwell, Oxford.

Pieter A. M. Seuren. 2004. *Chomsky's Minimalism*. Oxford University Press, Oxford.

Edward P. Stabler, Jr. 1992. Implementing government binding theories. In Robert Levine, editor, *Formal Grammar: Theory and Implementation*, pages 243–289. Oxford University Press, New York.

Mark Steedman. 2000. *The Syntactic Process*. MIT Press, Cambridge, MA.

Moshe Y. Vardi. 1982. The complexity of relational query languages. In *Proceedings of the 14th ACM Symposium on Theory of Computing*, pages 137–146, New York. Association for Computing Machinery.

Linguistics in Computational Linguistics: Observations and Predictions

Hans Uszkoreit
Language Technology Lab, DFKI GmbH
Stuhlsatzenhausweg 3, D-66123 Saarbruecken
uszkoreit@dfki.de

Abstract

As my title suggests, this position paper focuses on the relevance of linguistics in NLP instead of asking the inverse question. Although the question about the role of computational linguistics in the study of language may theoretically be much more interesting than the selected topic, I feel that my choice is more appropriate for the purpose and context of this workshop.

This position paper starts with some retrospective observations clarifying my view on the ambivalent and multi-facetted relationship between linguistics and computational linguistics as it has evolved from both applied and theoretical research on language processing. In four brief points I will then strongly advocate a strengthened relationship from which both sides benefit.

First, I will observe that recent developments in both deep linguistic processing and statistical NLP suggest a certain plausible division of labor between the two paradigms.

Second, I want to propose a systematic approach to research on hybrid systems which determines optimal combinations of the paradigms and continuously monitors the division of labor as both paradigm progress. Concrete examples illustrating the proposal are taken from our own research.

Third, I will argue that a central vision of computational linguistics is still alive, the dream of a formalized reusable linguistic knowledge source embodying the core competence of a language that can be utilized for wide range of applications.

1 Introduction

Computational linguistics did not organically grow out of linguistics as a new branch of mathematical or applied linguistics. Although the term suggests the association with linguistics, in practice much of CL has rather been purely engineering-driven natural language processing. Even if computational linguistics has become a recognized subfield of linguistics, most of the action in CL does not address linguistic research questions.

For most practitioners, the term was never more than a sexy sounding synonym for natural language processing. Many others, however, fortunately including many of the most creative and successful scientists in CL, shared the ambition of contributing to the scientific study of human language.

Already in the eighties Lauri Karttunen observed that there is a coexistence and mutual fertilization of applied computational linguistics and theoretical computational linguistics, and that the latter subarea can provide important insights into the structure and use of human language.

When we look into the actual relationship between linguistics and CL, we can easily perceive a number of changes that have happened over time. We can distinguish five major paradigms in computational linguistics, each of which has assigned a slightly different role to linguistic research. The first paradigm was the direct procedural implementation of language processing. NLP systems of this paradigm were programs in languages such as FORTRAN, COBOL or assembler in which there was no systematic division between linguistic knowledge and processing. Linguistics was only important because it had educated some of the practitioners on relevant properties of human language.

The second paradigm was the development of specialized algorithms and methods for language

Proceedings of the EACL 2009 Workshop on the Interaction between Linguistics and Computational Linguistics, pages 22–25,

processing. This paradigm includes for instance parsing algorithms, finite-state parsers, ATNs, RTNs and augmented phrase-structure grammars. Although we find a separation between linguistic knowledge and processing components, none of the developed methods were imports from linguistics, nor were they adopted in linguistics. (A notable exception may have been two-level finite-state morphology which at least caused some discussion in linguistic morphology.) Nevertheless, some of the approaches required a certain level of linguistic sophistication.

The third paradigm was the emergence of linguistic formalisms. In the eighties a variety of new declarative grammatical formalisms such as HPSG, LFG, CCG, CUG had quite some influence on CL. These formal grammar models were accompanied by semantic formalisms such as DRT. A number of these formal models were tightly connected to linguistic theories and therefore also taught in linguistics curricula. Several attempts to turn current versions of the linguistic mainstream theory of GB/P&P/minimalism into such a declarative formalism were not very successful in NLP but still discussed and used in linguistic classrooms.

When these linguistic formalisms failed to meet the performance criteria needed for realistic applications, most of applied computational linguistics research fell back on specialized methods for NLP such as finite state methods for information extraction. Other colleagues moved on to methods of the fourth paradigm in CL, i.e., statistical methods. Inspired by the rapid success of these statistical techniques, the new paradigm soon ruled most of NLP research. Not surprisingly, the distance between linguistics and mainstream CL increased, as researchers in most subareas researchers did not have to know much about language and linguistics in order to be successful in statistical NLP.

Only when the success curve of statistical NLP started to flatten in several application areas, interest in linguistic methods and knowledge sources reawakened. Hard core statistical NLP specialists consulted lexicons or tried to develop statistical models on phrase structures. Many statistical approaches now exploit structured linguistic descriptions as obtained from treebanks and other linguistically annotated corpora.

In the meantime, proponents of linguistic methods had discovered the power of statistical models for overcoming some of the performance limitations of deep NLP. Statistical models trained on treebanks have become the preferred method for solving the massive ambiguity problem of deep linguistic parsing.

All these pragmatic mixes of statistical and linguistic methods marked the birth of the fifth paradigm in CL, the creative combination of statistical and non-statistical machine learning approaches with linguistic methods.

2 Division of Labor between Linguistics and Statistics

To illustrate my view on the complementary contributions of statistical and linguistic methods I want to start with three observations. The first observation stems from parser evaluations. A CCG parser was successfully applied to the standard Wall Street Journal test data within the Penn Treebank (refs). Although the C&C parser did not quite get the same coverage as the best statistical systems, it produced very impressive results. As Mark Steedman demonstrated in a talk at the Computational Linguistics session of the 2008 International Congress of Linguists, the C&C parser moreover found many dependencies needed for semantic interpretation that are not even annotated in the Penn Treebank.

Observation two stems from our work on hybrid machine translation. Within the EU project EuroMatrix we are organizing open evaluation campaigns of MT systems by shared tasks whose results are reported in the annual WMT workshops. The first large campaign combining automatic and intellectual evaluation took place in 2008. Participants could contribute translations of two test data sets for a range of language pairs. One test set was in a specific domain for which training data had been provided. The other test set contained news texts on a variety of topics. Although a training set of news texts had been provided as well, the covered domains exhibited much more diversity than the closed domain texts. It turned out that in general the best systems for the closed domain task were statistical MT systems, whereas the open domain task was best solved by seasoned rule-based MT commercial products.

A careful comparative study of errors made by some of the best SMT and RBMT systems revealed that the errors of the two systems were largely complementary. As SMT can acquire frequently used expressions from training data, the output generally appears rather fluent, at least for short sentences and short portions of sentences. SMT is also superior in lexical and phrasal disambiguation and the optimal lexical choice in the target language. However, the translations exhibit many syntactic problems such as missing verbs or agreement violations, especially if the target language has a complex morphology. RBMT systems, on the other hand, usually get the syntactic structure right–unless they fail in attachment ambiguities–but on the word and phrase level they often do not select the correct or stylistically optimal translations.

Today's machine learning methods for acquiring the statistical translation models from parallel texts fail on many syntactic phenomena that can be analyzed correctly by a linguistic grammar. Inducing a correct treatment of long distance phenomena such as topicalization or "easy"-adjectives, ellipsis and control phenomena from unannotated texts seems quite impossible. Learning complex rules from syntactically and semantically annoted texts may be possible if linguists have already understood and formalized the underlying analysis of the phenomenon.

The third observation comes from supervising work in grammar development and attempts to enlarge the coverage of existing grammars automatically through the exploitation of corpus data. When he tried to extend the coverage of the ERG, Zhang Yi could show that almost all of the coverage gaps could be attributed to missing lexical knowledge. Even if the words in the unanalyzable sentence were all in the lexicon, usually some reading of words, i.e. their membership in some additional word class, was missing. The few remaining coverage deficits result from specific infrequent constructions not yet covered by the grammar plus missing treatments for a few notoriously tricky syntactic problems such as certain types of ellipsis.

These three observations together with numerous others strongly suggest the following insight. Every grammar of a human language consists of a small set of highly complex regularities and of a huge set of much less complex phenomena. The small set of highly complex phenomena occurs much more often than most of the phenomena of little complexity. This slanted distribution makes language learnable. So far we have no automatic learning methods that could correctly induce the complex phenomena. It is highly questionable whether these regularities could ever be induced without full access to the syntax-semantics mappings that the human language learner exploits.

On the other hand, the lexicon or simple selec-

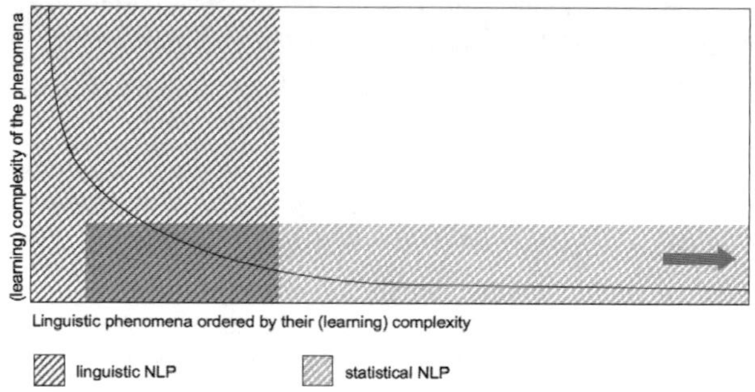

tional restrictions can easily be learned because the complexity lies in the structure of the lexical classes and not in the simple mapping from words to these classes.

3 Hybrid Systems Research

In several areas of language processing, first approaches of designing hybrid systems containing both linguistic and statistical components have demonstrated promising results.

However, much of this research is based on rather opportunistic selections. Readily available components are connected in a pure trial and error fashion. In our hybrid MT research we are systematically searching for optimal combinations of the best statistical and the best rule-based systems for a given language pair. The approach is systematic, because we use a detailed error analysis by skilled linguists to find out which classes of phrases are usually better translated by the best statistical systems. We then insert the translations for such kinds of phrases into the syntactic skeletons of the translated sentences provided by the rule-base system. One of the translations we submitted to this year's EuroMatrix evaluation campaign was obtained in this way.

The technique to merge sentence parts from the two systems into one translation is only a crude first approximation of a truly hybrid processing system, i.e., a system in which the statistical phrase translation is fully integrated into the rule-based system. Our goal is to test the usefulness of statistical methods in analysis, especially for disambiguation, in transfer, especially for selecting the best translation for words and smaller phrases and in generation, for the selection among paraphrases according to monolingual language models.

Another systematic approach to hybrid systems design was investigated in the Norwegian LOGON project, in which deep linguistic processing by HPSG and LFG was complemented by statistical methods.

Another example for a systematic approach to hybrid systems building is our work on an architecture for the combination of components for the analysis of texts. The DFKI platform Heart-of-Gold (HoG) was especially designed for this purpose. In HoG several components can be combined in multiple ways. All processing components write their analysis results into a multi-layer XML standoff annotation of the analyzed text. The actual interface language is RMRS (Robust Minimal Recursion Semantics, ref.) XML is just used as the syntactic carrier language for RMRS.

4 Computational Models of Linguistic Competence

Although the competence-performance distinction is a complex and highly controversial issue, the theoretical dichotomy is useful for the argument I want to make. When children acquire a language, they first learn to comprehend and produce spoken utterances. Much later they learn to read and to write, and much later again they may learn how to sing and rhyme and how to summarize, translate and proofread texts.

All of the acquired types of performance utilize their underlying linguistic competence. New types of performance are relatively easy to learn. The shared knowledge base ensures a useful level of consistency across the performance skills. Of course, each type of performance may use different parts of the shared competence. Certain types of performance may also extend the shared base into different directions.

The child could not acquire the complex mapping between sound and meaning without having access to both spoken (and later also written) form and the corresponding semantics. Therefore the child cannot learn a language from a radio beside her crib, nor can the older child acquire Chinese by being locked up in a library of Chinese books. Thus the basic competence cannot be obtained outside performance or successful communication.

The first approaches to linguistic computational grammars may have been too simplistic by not providing the connection between competence and performance needed for exploiting the competence base in realistic applications. However, in gradually solving the problems of efficiency, robustness and coverage researchers have arrived at more sophisticated views of deep linguistic processing.

After several decades of experience in working on competence and performance modeling for both generic grammatical resources and many specialized applications, I am fully convinced that the goal of a reusable shared competence model for every surviving language in our global digital information and communication structure is still a worthwhile and central goal of computational linguistics. I am also certain that the goal will be obtained in many steps. We already witness a reuse of large computational grammar resources such as the HPSG ERG, the LFG ParGram Grammar and the English CCG in many different applications. These applications are still experimental but when deep linguistic processing keeps improving in efficiency, specificity (ability to select among readings), robustness and coverage at current speed of progress, we will soon see first cases of real life applications.

I am not able to predict the respective proportions of the intellectually designed core components, the components learned automatically from linguistically annotated data and the components automatically learned from unannotated data but I am convinced that the systematic search for the best combinations will be central to partially realizing the dream of computational linguistics still within our life times.

If such solutions can be found and gradually improved, the insights gained through this systematic investigation may certainly also have a strong impact in the other direction, i.e. from computational linguistics into linguistics.

Linguistically Naïve != Language Independent: Why NLP Needs Linguistic Typology

Emily M. Bender
University of Washington
Seattle, WA, USA
ebender@u.washington.edu

Abstract

In this position paper, I argue that in order to create truly language-independent NLP systems, we need to incorporate linguistic knowledge. The linguistic knowledge in question is not intricate rule systems, but generalizations from linguistic typology about the range of variation in linguistic structures across languages.

1 Introduction

Language independence is commonly presented as one of the advantages of modern, machine-learning approaches to NLP. Once an algorithm is developed, the argument goes, it can trivially be extended to another language; "all" that is needed is a suitably large amount of training data for the new language.[1] This is indeed a virtue. However, the typical approach to developing language-independent systems is to eschew using any linguistic knowledge in their production. In this position paper, I argue that, on the contrary, the production of language-independent NLP technology *requires* linguistic knowledge, and that the relevant kind of linguistic knowledge is in fact relatively inexpensive.

The rest of this paper is structured as follows: In Section 2, I discuss how linguistically naïve systems can end up tuned to the languages they were originally developed for. In Section 3, I survey the long papers from ACL2008:HLT to give a snapshot of how linguistic diversity is currently handled in our field. In Section 4, I give a brief overview of Linguistic Typology, and suggest how knowledge derived from this field can be profitably incorporated into language-independent NLP systems.

2 Hidden Language Dependence

A simple example of subtle language dependence is the way in which n-gram models work better for languages that share important typological properties with English. On the face of it, n-gram models code in no linguistic knowledge. They treat natural language text as simple sequences of symbols and automatically reflect the "hidden" structure through the way it affects the distributions of words in various (flat, unstructured) contexts. However, the effectiveness of n-gram models in English (and similar languages) is partially predicated on two properties of those languages: relatively low levels of inflectional morphology, and relatively fixed word order.

As is well-known by now, languages with more elaborate morphology (more morphemes per word, more distinctions within the same number of morphological slots, and/or fewer uninflected words) present greater data sparsity problems for language models. This data sparsity limits the ability of n-gram models to capture the dependencies between open-class morphemes, but also closed class morphemes. The information expressed by short function words in English is typically expressed by the inflectional morphology in languages with more elaborate morphological systems. Word-based n-gram models have no way of representing the function morphemes in such a language. In addition, for n-gram models to capture inter-word dependencies, both words have to appear in the n-gram window. This will happen more consistently in languages with relatively fixed word order, as compared to languages with relatively free word order.

Thus even though n-grams models can be built

[1] This of course abstracts away from the production of such data, which may require both significant pre-processing and annotation work. For the purposes of the present argument, however, we can assume that all language-independent NLP systems are unicode-enabled, assume a definition of "word" that is cross-linguistically applicable, and require the type of annotations that are likely to have already been deployed for another purpose.

Proceedings of the EACL 2009 Workshop on the Interaction between Linguistics and Computational Linguistics, pages 26–32,
Athens, Greece, 30 March, 2009.

without any hand-coding of linguistic knowledge, they are not truly language independent. Rather, their success depends on typological properties of the languages they were first developed for. A more linguistically-informed (and thus more language independent) approach to n-gram models is the factored language model approach of Bilmes and Kirchhoff (2003). Factored language models address the problems of data-sparsity in morphologically complex languages by representing words as bundles of features, thus capturing dependencies between subword parts of adjacent words.

A second example of subtle language dependence comes from Dasgupta and Ng (2007), who present an unsupervised morphological segmentation algorithm meant to be language-independent. Indeed, this work goes much further towards language independence than is the norm (see Section 3). It is tested against data from English, Bengali, Finnish and Turkish, a particularly good selection of languages in that it includes diversity along a key dimension (degree of morphological complexity), as well as representatives of three language families (Indo-European, Uralic, and Altaic). Furthermore, the algorithm is designed to detect more than one prefix or suffix per word, which is important for analyzing morphologically complex languages. However, it seems unrealistic to expect a one-size-fits-all approach to be achieve uniformly high performance across varied languages, and, in fact, it doesn't. Though the system presented in (Dasgupta and Ng, 2007) outperforms the best systems in the 2006 PASCAL challenge for Turkish and Finnish, it still does significantly worse on these languages than English (F-scores of 66.2 and 66.5, compared to 79.4).

This seems to be due to an interesting interaction of at least two properties of the languages in question. First, the initial algorithm for discovering candidate roots and affixes relies on the presence of bare, uninflected roots in the training vocabulary, extracting a string as a candidate affix (or sequence of affixes) when it appears at the end (or beginning) of another string that also appears independently. In Turkish and Finnish, verbs appear as bare roots in many fewer contexts than in English.[2] This is also true in Bengali, and the authors note that their technique for detecting allomorphs is critical to finding "out-of-vocabulary" roots (those unattested as stand-alone words) in that language. However, the technique for finding allomorphs assumes that "roots exhibit the character changes during attachment, not suffixes" (p.160), and this is where another property of Finnish and Turkish becomes relevant: Both of these languages exhibit vowel harmony, where the vowels in many suffixes vary depending on the vowels of the root, even if consonants intervene. Thus I speculate that at least some of the reduced performance in Turkish and Finnish is due to the system not being able to recognize variants of the same suffixes as the same, and, in addition, not being able to isolate all of the roots.

Of course, in some cases, one language may represent, in some objective sense, a harder problem than another. A clear example of this is English letter-to-phoneme conversion, which, as a result of the lack of transparency in English orthography, is a harder problem that letter-to-phoneme conversion in other languages. Not surprisingly, the letter-to-phoneme systems described in e.g. (Jiampojamarn et al., 2008) and (Bartlett et al., 2008) do worse on the English test data than they do on German, Dutch, or French. On the other hand, just because one language may present a harder problem than the other doesn't mean that system developers can assume that any performance differences can be explained in such a way. If one aims to create a language-independent system, then one must explore the possibility that the system includes assumptions about linguistic structure which do not hold up across all languages.

The conclusions I would like to draw from these examples are as follows: A truly language-independent system works equally well across languages. When a system that is meant to be language independent does not in fact work equally well across languages, it is likely because something about the system design is making implicit assumptions about language structure. These assumptions are typically the result of "overfitting" to the original development language(s).[3] In Sec-

[2]In Finnish, depending on the verb class, the bare root may appear in negated present tense sentences, in second-person singular imperatives, and third-person singular present tense, or not at all (Karlsson and Chesterman, 1999). In Turkish, the bare root can function as a familiar imperative, but other forms are inflected (Lewis, 1967; Underhill, 1976).

[3]Here I use the term "overfitting" metaphorically, to call out the way in which, as the developers of NLP methodology, we rely on our intuitions about the structure of the language(s) we're working with and the feedback we get by test-

tion 4, I will argue that the best way to achieve language independence is by including, rather than eschewing, linguistic knowledge.

3 Language Independence and Language Representation at ACL

This section reports on a survey of the 119 long papers from ACL2008:HLT. Of these 119 papers, 18 explicitly claimed (16) or suggested (2) that the methods described could be applied to other languages. Another 13 could be read as implicitly claiming that. Still others present the kind of methodology that often is claimed to be cross-linguistically applicable, such as statistical machine translation. Of the 16 explicitly claiming language independence, 7 evaluated their systems on multiple languages. Since many of the techniques are meant to be cross-linguistically applicable, I collected information about the languages studied in all 119 papers. Table 1 groups the papers by how many languages (or language pairs) they study. The three papers studying zero languages involved abstract, formal proofs regarding, e.g., grammar formalisms. 95 of the papers studied just one language or language pair.

Languages or language pairs considered	Number of papers
0	3
1	95
2	13
3	3
4	2
5	1
12	1
13	1
Total	119

Table 1: Number of languages/language pairs considered

The two papers looking at the widest variety of languages were (Ganchev et al., 2008) and (Nivre and McDonald, 2008). Ganchev et al. (2008) explore whether better alignments lead to better translations, across 6 language pairs, in each direction (12 MT systems), collecting data from a variety of sources. Nivre and McDonald (2008) present an approach to dependency parsing which integrates graph-based and transition-based methods, and evaluate the result against the 13 datasets provided in the CoNLL-X shared task (Nivre et al., 2007).

ing our ideas against particular languages.

It is encouraging to see such use of multilingual datasets; the field as a whole will be in a better position to test (and improve) the cross-linguistic applicability of various methods to the extent that more such datasets are produced. It is worth noting, however, that the sheer number of languages tested is not the only important factor: Because related languages tend to share typological properties, it is also important to sample across the known language *families*.

Tables 2 and 3 list the languages and language pairs studied in the papers in the survey. Table 2 presents the data on methodologies that involve producing results for one language at a time, and groups the languages by genus and family (according to the classification used by the World Atlas of Language Structures Online[4]). Table 3 presents the data on methodologies that involve symmetrical (e.g., bilingual lexicon extraction) or asymmetrical (e.g., MT) language pairs.[5]

The first thing to note in these tables is the concentration of work on English: 63% of the single-language studies involved English, and all of the language pairs studied included English as one member. In many cases, the authors did not explicitly state which language they were working on. That it was in fact English could be inferred from the data sources cited, in some cases, or from the examples used, in others. The common practice of not explicitly stating the language when it is English would seem to follow from a general sense that the methods should be crosslinguistically applicable.

The next thing to note about these tables is that many of the languages included are close relatives of each other. Ethnologue[6] lists 94 language families; ACL2008:HLT papers studied six. Of course, the distribution of languages (and perhaps more to the point, speakers) is not uniform across lan-

[4]http://wals.info (Haspelmath et al., 2008); Note that Japanese is treated as a language isolate and Chinese is the name for the genus including (among others) Mandarin and Cantonese.

[5]The very interesting study by Snyder and Barzilay (2008) on multilingual approaches to morphological segmentation was difficult to classify. Their methodology involved jointly analyzing two languages at a time in order to produce morphological segmenters for each. Since the resulting systems were monolingual, the data from these studies are included in Table 2.

[6]http://www.ethnologue.com/ethno_docs/distribution.asp, accessed on 6 February 2009.

Language	Studies		Genus	Studies		Family	Studies	
	N	%		N	%		N	%
English	81	63.28	Germanic	91	71.09	Indo-European	109	85.16
German	5	3.91						
Dutch	3	2.34						
Danish	1	0.78						
Swedish	1	0.78						
Czech	3	2.34	Slavic	8	6.25			
Russian	2	1.56						
Bulgarian	1	0.78						
Slovene	1	0.78						
Ukranian	1	0.78						
Portuguese	3	2.34	Romance	8	6.25			
Spanish	3	2.34						
French	2	1.56						
Hindi	2	1.56	Indic	2	1.56			
Arabic	4	3.13	Semitic	9	7.03	Afro-Asiatic	9	7.03
Hebrew	4	3.13						
Aramaic	1	0.78						
Chinese	5	3.91	Chinese	5	3.91	Sino-Tibetan	5	3.91
Japanese	3	2.34	Japanese	3	3.24	Japanese	3	3.24
Turkish	1	0.78	Turkic	1	0.78	Altaic	1	0.78
Wambaya	1	0.78	West Barkly	1	0.78	Australian	1	0.78
Total	128	100.00		128	100.00		128	100.00

Table 2: Languages studied in ACL 2008 papers, by language genus and family

Source	Target	N	Source	Target	N	Symmetrical pair	N
Chinese	English	9	English	Chinese	2	English, Chinese	3
Arabic	English	5	English	Arabic	2	English, Arabic	1
French	English	2	English	French	2	English, French	1
Czech	English	1	English	Czech	2	English, Spanish	1
Finnish	English	1	English	Finnish	1		
German	English	1	English	German	1		
Italian	English	1	English	Italian	1		
Spanish	English	1	English	Spanish	1		
			English	Greek	1		
			English	Russian	1		

Table 3: Language pairs studied in ACL 2008 papers

Language family	Living lgs.	Examples	% pop.
Indo-European	430	Welsh Pashto Bengali	44.78
Sino-Tibetan	399	Mandarin Sherpa Burmese	22.28
Niger-Congo	1,495	Swahili Wolof Bissa	6.26
Afro-Asiatic	353	Arabic Coptic Somali	5.93
Austronesian	1,246	Bali Tagalog Malay	5.45
Total	3,923		84.7

Table 4: Six most populous language families, from Ethnologue

guage families. Table 4 gives the five most populous language families, again from Ethnologue.[7] These language families together account for almost 85% of the world's population.

Of course, language independence is not the only motivation for machine-learning approaches to NLP. Others include scaling to different genres within a language, robustness in the face of noisy input, the argument (in some cases) that creating or obtaining training data is cheaper than creating a rule-based system, and the difficulty in certain tasks of creating rule-based systems. Nonetheless, to the extent that language independence is an important goal, the field needs to improve both its testing of language independence and its sampling of languages to test against.

4 Linguistic Knowledge

Typically, when we think of linguistic knowledge-based NLP systems, what comes to mind are complicated, intricate sets of language-specific rules. While I would be the last to deny that such systems can be both linguistically interesting and the best approach to certain tasks, my purpose here is to point out that there are other kinds of linguistic knowledge that can be fruitfully incorporated into NLP systems. In particular, the results of language typology represent a rich source of knowledge that, by virtue of being already produced by the typologists, can be relatively inexpensively incorporated into NLP systems.

Linguistic typology is an approach to the scientific study of language which was pioneered in its modern form by Joseph Greenberg in the 1950s and 1960s (see e.g. Greenberg, 1963).[8] In the intervening decades, it has evolved from a search for language universals and the limits of language variation to what Bickel (2007) characterizes as the study of "what's where why". That is, typologists are interested in how variations on particular linguistic phenomena are distributed throughout the world's languages, both in terms of language families and geography, and how those distributions came to be the way they are.

For the purposes of improving language-independent NLP systems, we are primarily concerned with "what" and "where": Knowing "what" (how languages can vary) allows us to both broaden and parameterize our systems. Knowing "where" also helps with parameterizing, as well as with selecting appropriate samples of languages to test the systems against. We can broaden them by studying what typologists have to say about our initial development languages, and identifying those characteristics we might be implicitly relying on. This is effectively what Bilmes and Kirchhoff (2003) did in generalizing n-gram language models to factored language models. We can parameterize our systems by identifying and specifically accommodating relevant language types ("what") and then using databases produced by typologists to map specific input languages to types ("where").

The practical point of language independence is not to be able to handle in principle any possible language in the universe (human or extraterrestrial!), but to improve the scalability of NLP technology across the existing set of human languages. There are approximately 7,000 languages spoken today, of which 347 have more than 1 million speakers.[9] An NLP system that uses different parameters or algorithms for each one of a set

[7]Ibid. Example languages are included to give the reader a sense of where these language families are spoken, and are deliberately chosen to represent the breadth of each language family while still being relatively recognizable to the EACL audience.

[8]See (Ramat, to appear) for discussion of much earlier approaches.

[9]http://wwww.ethnologue.com/ethno_docs/distribution.asp; accessed 6 February 2009

of known languages is not language independent. One that uses different parameters or even algorithms for different language *types*, and includes as a first step the classification of the input language, either automatically or with reference to some external typological database, *is* language independent, at least on the relevant, practical sense.

The preeminent typological database among those which are currently publicly available is WALS: The World Atlas of Linguistic Structures Online (Haspelmath et al., 2008). WALS currently includes studies of 142 chapters studying linguistic features, each of which defines a dimension of classification, describes values along that dimension, and then classifies a large sample of languages. It is also possible to view the data on a language-by-language basis. These chapters represent concise summaries, as well as providing pointers into the relevant literature for more information.

To give a sense of how this information might be of relevance to NLP or speech systems, here is a brief overview of three chapters:

Maddieson (2008) studies tone, or the use of pitch to differentiate words or inflectional categories. He classifies languages into those with no tone systems, those with simple tone systems (a binary contrast between high and low tone), and those with more complex tone systems (more than two tone types). Nearly half of the languages in the sample have some tone, and Maddieson points out that the sample in fact underestimates the number of languages with tone.

Dryer (2008b) investigates prefixing and suffixing in inflectional morphology, looking at 10 common types of affixes (from case affixes on nouns to adverbial subordinator affixes on verbs), and using them to classify languages in terms of tendencies towards prefixing or suffixing.[10] His resulting categories are: little affixation, strongly suffixing, weakly suffixing, equal prefixing and suffixing, weakly prefixing, and strongly prefixing. The most common category (382/894 languages) is predominantly suffixing.

Dryer (2008a) investigates the expression of clausal negation. One finding of note is that all languages studied use dedicated morphemes to express negation. This contrasts with the expression of yes-no questions which can be handled with word order changes, intonation, or no overt mark at all. The types of expression of clausal negation that Dryer identifies are: negative affix, negative auxiliary verb, and negative particle. In addition, some languages are classified as using a negative word that may be a verb or may be a particle, as having variation between negative affixes and negative words, and as having double (or two-part) negation, where each negative clause requires two markers, one before the verb, and one after it.

These examples illustrate several useful aspects of the knowledge systematized by linguistic typology: First, languages show variation beyond that which one might imagine looking only at a few familiar (and possibly closely related) languages. Second, however, that variation is still bounded: Though typologists are always interested in finding new categories that stretch the current classification, for the purposes of computational linguistics, we can get very far by assuming the known types exhaust the possibilities. Finally, because of the work done by field linguists and typologists, this knowledge is available as high-level generalizations about languages, of the sort that can inform the design of linguistically-sophisticated, language-independent NLP systems.

5 Conclusion

This paper has briefly argued that the best way to create language-independent systems is to include linguistic knowledge, specifically knowledge about the ways in which languages vary in their structure. Only by doing so can we ensure that our systems are not overfitted to the development languages. Furthermore, this knowledge is relatively inexpensive to incorporate, as it does not require building or maintaining intricate rule systems. Finally, if the field as a whole values language independence as a property of NLP systems, then we should ensure that the languages we select to use in evaluations are representative of both the language types and language families we are interested in.

Acknowledgments

I am grateful to Stephan Oepen and Timothy Baldwin for helpful discussion. Any remaining infelicities are my own. This material is based in part upon work supported by the National Science Foundation under Grant No. 0644097. Any opinions, findings, and conclusions or recommenda-

[10]For the purposes of this study, he sets aside less common inflectional strategies such as infixing, tone changes, and stem changes.

tions expressed in this material are those of the author and do not necessarily reflect the views of the National Science Foundation.

References

Susan Bartlett, Grzegorz Kondrak, and Colin Cherry. 2008. Automatic syllabification with structured SVMs for letter-to-phoneme conversion. In *Proceedings of ACL-08: HLT*, pages 568–576, Columbus, Ohio, June. Association for Computational Linguistics.

Balthasar Bickel. 2007. Typology in the 21st centure: Major current developments. *Linguistic Typology*, pages 239–251.

Jeff A. Bilmes and Katrin Kirchhoff. 2003. Factored language models and generalized parallel backoff. In *in Proceedings of HLT/NACCL, 2003*, pages 4–6.

Sajib Dasgupta and Vincent Ng. 2007. High-performance, language-independent morphological segmentation. In *Human Language Technologies 2007: The Conference of the North American Chapter of the Association for Computational Linguistics; Proceedings of the Main Conference*, pages 155–163, Rochester, New York, April. Association for Computational Linguistics.

Matthew S. Dryer. 2008a. Negative morphemes. In Martin Haspelmath, Matthew S. Dryer, David Gil, and Bernard Comrie, editors, *The World Atlas of Language Structures Online*. Max Planck Digital Library, Munich. Available online at http://wals.info/feature/112. Accessed on 2009-02-07.

Matthew S. Dryer. 2008b. Prefixing vs. suffixing in inflectional morphology. In Martin Haspelmath, Matthew S. Dryer, David Gil, and Bernard Comrie, editors, *The World Atlas of Language Structures Online*. Max Planck Digital Library, Munich. Available online at http://wals.info/feature/26. Accessed on 2009-02-07.

Kuzman Ganchev, João V. Graça, and Ben Taskar. 2008. Better alignments = better translations? In *Proceedings of ACL-08: HLT*, pages 986–993, Columbus, Ohio, June. Association for Computational Linguistics.

Joseph Greenberg. 1963. Some universals of grammar with particular reference to the order of meaningful elements. In *Univerals of Language*, pages 73–113. MIT Press, Cambridge.

Martin Haspelmath, Matthew S. Dryer, David Gil, and Bernard Comrie, editors. 2008. *The World Atlas of Language Structures Online*. Max Planck Digital Library, Munich. http://wals.info.

Sittichai Jiampojamarn, Colin Cherry, and Grzegorz Kondrak. 2008. Joint processing and discriminative training for letter-to-phoneme conversion. In *Proceedings of ACL-08: HLT*, pages 905–913, Columbus, Ohio, June. Association for Computational Linguistics.

Fred Karlsson and Andrew Chesterman. 1999. *Finnish: An Essential Grammar*. Routledge, London.

Geoffrey Lewis. 1967. *Turkish Grammar*. Clarendon Press, Oxford.

Ian Maddieson. 2008. Tone. In Martin Haspelmath, Matthew S. Dryer, David Gil, and Bernard Comrie, editors, *The World Atlas of Language Structures Online*. Max Planck Digital Library, Munich. Available online at http://wals.info/feature/13. Accessed on 2009-02-07.

Joakim Nivre and Ryan McDonald. 2008. Integrating graph-based and transition-based dependency parsers. In *Proceedings of ACL-08: HLT*, pages 950–958, Columbus, Ohio, June. Association for Computational Linguistics.

Joakim Nivre, Johan Hall, Sandra Kübler, Ryan McDonald, Jens Nilsson, Sebastian Riedel, and Deniz Yuret. 2007. The CoNLL 2007 shared task on dependency parsing. In *Proceedings of the CoNLL Shared Task Session of EMNLP-CoNLL 2007*, pages 915–932, Prague, Czech Republic, June. Association for Computational Linguistics.

Paolo Ramat. to appear. The (early) history of linguistic typology. In *The Oxford Handbook of Linguistic Typology*. Oxford University Press, Oxford.

Benjamin Snyder and Regina Barzilay. 2008. Unsupervised multilingual learning for morphological segmentation. In *Proceedings of ACL-08: HLT*, pages 737–745, Columbus, Ohio, June. Association for Computational Linguistics.

Robert Underhill. 1976. *Turkish Grammar*. MIT Press, Cambridge, MA.

Parsed Corpora for Linguistics

Gertjan van Noord
University of Groningen
G.J.M.van.noord@rug.nl

Gosse Bouma
University of Groningen
G.Bouma@rug.nl

Abstract

Knowledge-based parsers are now accurate, fast and robust enough to be used to obtain syntactic annotations for very large corpora fully automatically. We argue that such parsed corpora are an interesting new resource for linguists. The argument is illustrated by means of a number of recent results which were established with the help of parsed corpora.

1 Introduction

Once upon a time, knowledge-based parsers were slow, inaccurate and fragile. This is no longer true. In the last decade, enormous improvements have been achieved in this area. Parsers based on constraint-based formalisms such as HPSG, LFG, and CCG are now fast enough for many applications; they are robust; and they perform much more accurately than previously by incorporating, typically, a statistical disambiguation component. As a consequence, such parsers now obtain competitive, if not superior, performance. Zaenen (2004), for instance, points out that the (LFG-based) XLE parser is fast, has a statistical disambiguation component, and is robust, and thus allows full parsing to be incorporated in many applications. Clark and Curran (2007) show that both accurate and highly efficient parsing is possible using a CCG.

As a consequence of this development, massive amounts of parsed sentences now become available. Such large collections of syntactically annotated but not manually verified syntactic analyses are a very useful resource for many purposes. In this position paper we focus on one purpose: linguistic analysis. Our claim is, that very large *parsed* corpora are an important resource for linguists. Such very large parsed corpora can be used to search systematically for specific infrequent syntactic configurations of interest, and also to obtain quantitative data about specific syntactic configurations. Although parsed corpora obviously contain a certain amount of noise, for many applications the abundant size of these corpora compensates for this.

In this paper, we illustrate our position by a numer of recent linguistic studies in which very large corpora of Dutch have been employed, which were syntactically annotated by the freely available Alpino parser (Bouma et al., 2001; van Noord, 2006).

The Alpino system incorporates a linguistically motivated, wide-coverage grammar for Dutch in the tradition of HPSG. It consists of over 800 grammar rules and a large lexicon of over 300,000 lexemes (including very many person names, geographical names, and organization names) and various rules to recognize special constructs such as named entities, temporal expressions, etc. Since we use Alpino to parse large amounts of data, it is crucial that the parser is capable to treat sentences with unknown words. A large set of heuristics have been implemented carefully to deal with unknown words and word sequences.

Based on the categories assigned to words, and the set of grammar rules compiled from the HPSG grammar, a left-corner parser finds the set of all parses, and stores this set compactly in a packed parse forest. All parses are rooted by an instance of the top category, which is a category that generalizes over all maximal projections (S, NP, VP, ADVP, AP, PP and some others). If there is no parse covering the complete input, the parser finds all parses for each substring. In such cases, the robustness component will then select the best sequence of non-overlapping parses (i.e., maximal projections) from this set.

In order to select the best parse from the parse forest, a best-first search algorithm is applied. The algorithm consults a Maximum Entropy disambiguation model to judge the quality of (partial)

Proceedings of the EACL 2009 Workshop on the Interaction between Linguistics and Computational Linguistics, pages 33–39,
Athens, Greece, 30 March, 2009.

parses. The disambiguation model is trained on the manually verified Alpino treebank (about 7100 sentences from newspaper texts).

Although Alpino is not a dependency grammar in the traditional sense, dependency structures are generated by the lexicon and grammar rules as the value of a dedicated feature. The dependency structures are based on CGN (Corpus Gesproken Nederlands, Corpus of Spoken Dutch) (Hoekstra et al., 2003), D-Coi and LASSY (van Noord et al., 2006).

Dependency structures are stored in XML. Advantages of the use of XML include the availability of general purpose search and visualization software. For instance, we exploit XPATH (standard XML query language) to search in large sets of dependency structures, and Xquery to extract information from such large sets of dependency structures (Bouma and Kloosterman, 2002; Bouma and Kloosterman, 2007).

2 Extraposition of comparative objects out of topic

The first illustration of our thesis that parsed corpora provide an interesting new resource for linguists, constitutes more of an anecdote than a systematic study. We include the example, presented earlier in van Noord (2009), because it is fairly easy to explain, and because it was how we became aware ourselves of the potential of parsed corpora for the purpose of linguistics.

In van der Beek et al. (2002), the grammar underlying the Alpino parser is presented in some detail. As an example of how the various specific rules of the grammar interact with the more general principles, the analysis of comparatives and the interaction with generic principles for (rightward) extraposition is illustrated. In short, comparatives such as comparative adjectives and the adverb `anders` as in the following example (1) license corresponding comparative phrases (such as phrases headed by `dan` (than)) by means of a feature which percolates according to the extraposition principle. The analysis is illustrated in figure 1.

(1) ... niks anders doen dan almaar
... nothing else do than continuously
ruw materiaal verzamelen
raw material collect
do nothing else but collect raw material (cdbl-7)

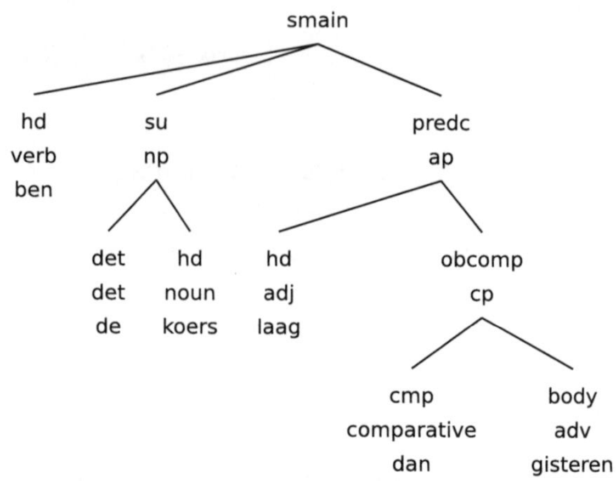

Figure 2: Dependency structure for *Lager was de koers dan gisteren*

An anonymous reviewer criticized the analysis, because the extraposition principle would also allow the rightward extraction of comparative phrases licensed by comparatives in topic position. The extraposition principle would have to allow for this in the light of examples such as

(2) De vraag is gerechtvaardigd waarom de
The question is justified why the
regering niets doet
government nothing does
The question is justified why the goverment does not act

However, the reviewer claimed that comparative phrases cannot be extraposed out of topic, as examples such as the following indicate:

(3) *Lager was de koers dan gisteren
Lower was the rate than yesterday
The rate never was lower than yesterday

Since the Alpino grammar allows such cases, it is possible to investigate if genuine examples of this type occur in parsed corpora. In order to understand how we can specify a search query for such cases, it is instructive to consider the dependency structure assigned to such examples in figure 2. As can be observed in the dependency graph, the left-right order of nodes does not represent the left-right ordering in the sentence. The word-order of words and phrases is indicated with XML attributes *begin* and *end* (not shown in figure 2) which indicate for each node the begin and end position in the sentence respectively.

The following XPATH query enumerates all ex-

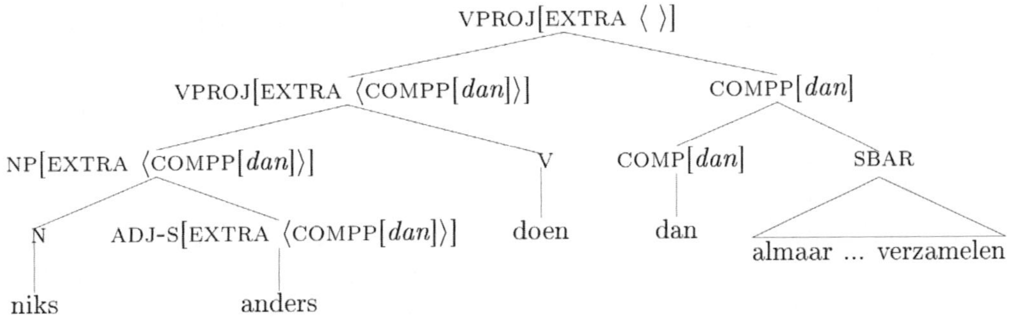

Figure 1: Derivation of extraposed comparative object

amples of extraposition of comparative phrases out of topic. We can then inspect the resulting list to check whether the examples are genuine.

```
//node[
  @cat="smain"
  and
  node[
    node[@rel="obcomp"]/@end
    >
    ../node[@rel="hd"]/@begin
      ]/@begin = @begin
     ]
```

The query can be read as: find root sentences in which there is a daughter node, which itself has a daughter node with relation label `obcomp` (the label used for comparative complements). The daughter node should begin at the same position as the root sentence. Finally, the end position of the `obcomp` node must be larger than the end position of the head of the root sentence (i.e. the finite verb).

In addition to many mis-parsed sentences, we found quite a few genuine cases. A mis-parse can for instance occur if a sentence contains two potential licensers for the comparative phrase, as in the following example in which *verder* can be wrongly analysed as a comparative adjective.

(4) Verder wil ik dat mijn backhand even
Further want I that my backhand just-as
goed wordt als mijn forehand
good becomes as my forehand
Furthermore, I want my backhand to become as good as my forehand

More interestingly for the present discussion are the examples which were parsed correctly. Not only do we find such examples, but informants agree that nothing is wrong with such cases. Some examples are listed in figure 3. It is striking that many examples involve the comparative adjectives *liever* and *eerder*. Also, the list involves examples where adverbials such as *zo, zozeer, zoveel* are related with an extraposed subordinate sentence headed by *dat* which according to the annotation guidelines are also treated as comparative complements.

The examples show that at least in some cases, the possibility of extraposition of comparative complements out of topic must be allowed; we hypothesize that the acceptability of such cases is not a binary decision, but rather a preference which depends on the choice of comparative on the one hand, and the heaviness of the comparative complement on the other hand.

For the purpose of this paper, we hope to have illustrated how parsed corpora can be helpful to find new empirical evidence for fairly complicated and suble linguistic issues. Note that for a construction of this type, manually verified treebanks are much too small. We estimated that it takes about 5 million words to find a single, good, example. It appears unrealistic to assume that treebanks of the required order of magnitude of tens of millions of words will become available soon.

3 Frequency versus Complexity

Our second illustration is of a different nature, and taken from a study related to agrammatic Broca's aphasia.

In Bastiaanse et al. (to appear), potential causes are discussed of the problems that patients suffering from agrammatic Broca's aphasia encounter. The *Derived Order Problem Hypothesis* (Bastiaanse and van Zonneveld, 2005) assumes that the linguistic representations of agrammatic patients are intact, but due to processing disorders, some representations are harder to retrieve than oth-

(5) Liever betaalden werkgevers een (hoge) verzekeringspremie , dan opgescheept te zitten met niet
Rather paid employers a (high) insurance-fee , than left to be with not
volwaardig functionerende medewerkers
fully functioning employees
Rather, employers pay a high insurance fee, than be left with not fully functioning employees (Algemeen Dagblad, January 15, 1999)

(6) Beter is het te zorgen dat ziekenhuizen hun verplichtingen volgens de huidige BOPZ gaan
Better is it to ensure that hospitals their obligations according-to the current BOPZ start
nakomen , dan de rechten van patiï¿½ten nog verder aan te tasten
meet , than the rights of patients yet further PART to violate
It is better to ensure that hospitals start to meet their obligations according to the current BOZP, than to violate rights of patients even further (Algemeen Dagblad, August 18, 2001)

(7) Dus wat anders konden de LPF'ers de afgelopen week dan zich stil houden ?
So what else could the LPF-representatives the last week than self quiet keep ?
What else could the LPF-representatives do last week , than keep quiet? (Volkskrant June 1, 2002)

(8) Sneller kennen ze hun tafels van vermenigvuldiging dan de handelingen van de groet
Faster know they their tables of multiplication than the acts of the greeting
They know the tables of multiplication faster than the acts of greeting (De Morgen March 27, 2006)

Figure 3: Some genuine examples of extraposition of comparative objects from topic. The examples are identified automatically using an XPATH query applied to a large parsed corpus.

ers, due to differences in linguistic complexity. This hypothesis thus assumes that agrammatic patients have difficulty with constructions of higher linguistic complexity. An alternative hypothesis states, that agrammatic patients have more difficulty with linguistic constructions of lower frequency.

In order to compare the two hypotheses, Bastiaanse *et al.* perform three corpus studies. In three earlier experimental studies it was found that agrammatic patients have more difficulty with (a) finite verbs in verb-second position versus finite verbs in verb-final position; (b) scrambled direct objects versus non-scrambled direct objects; and (c) transitive verbs used as unaccusative versus transitive verbs used as transitive.

The three pairs of constructions are illustrated as follows.

(9) a. de jongen die een boek leest
the boy who a book reads
the boy who reads a book
b. de jongen leest een boek
the boy reads a book
the boy reads a book

(10) a. dit is de jongen die vandaag het boek leest
this is the boy who today the book reads
this is the boy who reads the book today
b. dit is de jongen die het boek vandaag leest
this is the boy who the book today reads
this is the boy who reads the book today

(11) a. de jongen breekt het glas
the boy breaks the glass
the boy breaks the glass
b. het glas breekt
the glass breaks
the glass breaks

In each of the three cases, corpus data is used to estimate the frequency of both syntactic configurations. Two corpora were used: the manually verified syntactically annotated CGN corpus (spoken language, approx. 1M words), and the the automatically parsed TwNC corpus (Ordelman et al., 2007) (the newspapers up to 2001, a parsed corpus of 300 million words). For the first two experiments, manual inspection revealed that the parsed corpus material was of high enough quality to be used directly. Furthermore, the relevant constructions are highly frequent, and thus even relatively small corpora (such as the syntactically annotated part of CGN) provide sufficient data. For the third experiment (unaccusative versus transitive usage of verbs), an additional layer of manual verification was used, and furthermore, as the subcategorization frequencies of individual verbs are estimated, the full TwNC was searched in order to obtain reasonably reliable estimates.

The outcome of the three experiments was the same in each case: frequency information cannot explain the difficulty encountered by agrammatic patients. Verb-second is more frequent than verb-final word order for lexical verbs and transitive lexical verbs (the verbs used in the experiments were all transitive). Finite verbs occur slightly more often in verb-second position than in verb-final position, but the difference is quite small. Scrambled word order is more frequent than the basic word order. The difference between the two corpora (CGN and TwNC) is quite small in both cases. Figure 4 gives an overview of the number of occurrences of the transitive and unaccusative use of the verbs used in the experiments in the full TwNC. The data suggest that the relative frequency of unaccusative depends strongly on the verb, but that it is not in general the case that the unaccusative use is less frequent than the transitive use.

The three 'difficult' constructions used in the experiments with aphasia patients are by no means infrequent in Dutch. The authors conclude that the hypothesis that processing difficulties are correlated with higher linguistic complexity cannot be falsified by an appeal to frequency.

What is interesting for the purposes of the current paper, is that parsed corpora are used to estimate frequencies of syntactic constructions, and that these are used to support claims about the role of linguistic complexity in processing difficulties of aphasia patients. Also note that figure 4 shows that even in a large (300M word) corpus, the number of occurrences of a specific verb used with a specific valency frame can be quite small. Thus, it is unlikely that reliable frequency estimates can be obtained for these cases from manually verified treebanks.

Roland et al. (2007) report on closely related work for English. In particular, they give frequency counts for a range of syntactic constructions in English, and subcategorization frequencies for specific verbs. They demonstrate that these frequencies are highly dependent on corpus and genre in a number of cases. They use their data to verify claims in the psycholinguistic literature about the processing of subject vs. object clefts, relative clauses and sentential complements.

4 The distribution of *zelf* and *zichzelf*

As a further example of the use of parsed corpora to further linguistic insights, we consider a recent study (Bouma and Spenader, 2009) of the distribution of weak and strong reflexive objects in Dutch.

If a verb is used reflexively in Dutch, two forms of the reflexive pronoun are available. This is illustrated for the third person form in the examples below.

(12) Brouwers schaamt **zich/*zichzelf** voor zijn
Brouwers shames *self1/self2* for his
schrijverschap.
writing
Brouwers is ashamed of his writing

(13) Duitsland volgt ***zich/zichzelf** niet op
Germany follows *self1/self2* not PART
als Europees kampioen.
as European Champion
Germany does not succeed itself as European champion

(14) Wie **zich/zichzelf** niet juist
Who self1/self2 not properly
introduceert, valt af.
introduces, is out
Everyone who does not introduce himself properly, is out.

The choice between *zich* and *zichzelf* depends on the verb. Generally three groups of verbs are distinguished. Inherent reflexives are claimed to never occur with a non-reflexive argument, and as a reflexive argument are claimed to use *zich* exclusively, (12). Non-reflexive verbs seldom, if ever occur with a reflexive argument. If they do however, they can only take *zichzelf* as a reflexive argument (13). Accidental reflexives can be used with both *zich* and *zichzelf*, (14). Accidental reflexive verbs vary widely as to the frequency with which they occur with both arguments. Bouma and Spenader (2009) set out to explain this distribution.

The influential theory of Reinhart and Reuland (1993) explains the distribution as the surface realization of two different ways of reflexive coding. An accidental reflexive that can be realized with

verb		unacc #	unacc %	trans #	trans %
luiden	*to ring/sound*	269	26.6	743	73.4
scheuren	*to rip*	332	28.8	819	71.2
breken	*to break*	1969	31.2	4341	68.8
verbrand	*to burn*	479	43.5	623	56.5
oplossen	*to (dis)solve*	296	59.2	204	40.8
draaien	*to turn*	2709	59.4	1852	40.6
smelten	*to melt*	723	71.4	290	28.6
rollen	*to roll*	3500	93.5	244	6.5
verdrinken	*to drown*	1397	94.6	80	5.4
stuiteren	*to bounce*	334	97.9	7	2.1

Figure 4: Estimated number of occurrences in TwNC of unaccusative and transitive uses of Dutch verbs which may undergo the causative alternation

both *zich* and *zichzelf* is actually ambiguous between an inherent reflexive and an accidental reflexive (which always is realized with *zichzelf*). An alternative approach is that of Haspelmath (2004), Smits et al. (2007), and Hendriks et al. (2008), who have claimed that the distribution of weak vs. strong reflexive object pronouns correlates with the proportion of events described by the verb that are self-directed vs. other-directed.

In the course of this investigation, a first interesting observation is, that many inherently reflexive verbs, which are claimed not to occur with *zichzelf*, actually often do combine with this pronoun. Here are a number of examples (simplified for expository purposes):

(15) Nederland moet stoppen zichzelf op de
Netherlands must stop self2 on the
borst te slaan
chest to beat
The Netherlands must stop beating itself on the chest

(16) Hunze wil zichzelf niet al te zeer op
Hunze want self2 not all too much on
de borst kloppen
the chest knock
Hunze doesn't want to knock itself on the chest too much

(17) Ze verloren zichzelf soms in het
They lost self2 sometimes in tactical
gegoochel met allerlei tactische varianten
variants
They sometimes lost themselves in tactical variants

With regards to the main hypothesis of their study, (Bouma and Spenader, 2009) use linear regression to determine the correlation between reflexive use of a (non-inherently reflexive) verb and the relative preference for a weak or strong reflexive pronoun. Frequency counts are collected from the parsed TwNC corpus (almost 500 million words). They limit the analysis to verbs that occur at least 10 times with a reflexive meaning and at least 50 times in total, distinguishing uses by subcategorization frames. The statistical analysis shows a significant correlation, which accounts for 30% of the variance of the ratio of nonreflexive over reflexive uses.

5 Conclusion

Knowledge-based parsers are now accurate, fast and robust enough to be used to obtain syntactic annotations for very large corpora fully automatically. We argued that such parsed corpora are an interesting new resource for linguists. The argument is illustrated by means of a number of recent results which were established with the help of huge parsed corpora.

Huge parsed corpora are especially crucial (1) to obtain evidence concerning infrequent syntactic configurations, and (2) to obtain more reliable quantitative data about particular syntactic configurations.

Acknowledgments

This research was carried out in part in the context of the STEVIN programme which is funded by the Dutch and Flemish governments (http://taalunieversum.org/taal/technologie/stevin/).

References

Roelien Bastiaanse and Ron van Zonneveld. 2005. Sentence production with verbs of alternating transitivity in agrammatic Broca's aphasia. *Journal of Neurolinguistics*, 18(1):57–66, January.

Roelien Bastiaanse, Gosse Bouma, and Wendy Post. to appear. Frequency and linguistic complexity in agrammatic speech production. *Brain and Language*.

Gosse Bouma and Geert Kloosterman. 2002. Querying dependency treebanks in XML. In *Proceedings of the Third international conference on Language Resources and Evaluation (LREC)*, pages 1686–1691, Gran Canaria, Spain.

Gosse Bouma and Geert Kloosterman. 2007. Mining syntactically annotated corpora using XQuery. In *Proceedings of the Linguistic Annotation Workshop*, Prague, June. ACL.

Gosse Bouma and Jennifer Spenader. 2009. The distribution of weak and strong object reflexives in Dutch. In Frank van Eynde, Anette Frank, Koenraad De Smedt, and Gertjan van Noord, editors, *Proceedings of the Seventh International Workshop on Treebanks and Linguistic Theories (TLT 7)*, number 12 in LOT Occasional Series, pages 103–114, Utrecht, The Netherlands. Netherlands Graduate School of Linguistics.

Gosse Bouma, Gertjan van Noord, and Robert Malouf. 2001. Wide coverage computational analysis of Dutch. In W. Daelemans, K. Sima'an, J. Veenstra, and J. Zavrel, editors, *Computational Linguistics in the Netherlands 2000*.

S. Clark and J.R. Curran. 2007. Wide-Coverage Efficient Statistical Parsing with CCG and Log-Linear Models. *Computational Linguistics*, 33(4):493–552.

Martin Haspelmath. 2004. A frequentist explanation of some universals of reflexive marking. Draft of a paper presented at the Workshop on Reciprocals and Reflexives, Berlin.

Petra Hendriks, Jennifer Spenader, and Erik-Jan Smits. 2008. Frequency-based constraints on reflexive forms in Dutch. In *Proceedings of the 5th International Workshop on Constraints and Language Processing*, pages 33–47, Roskilde, Denmark.

Heleen Hoekstra, Michael Moortgat, Bram Renmans, Machteld Schouppe, Ineke Schuurman, and Ton van der Wouden, 2003. *CGN Syntactische Annotatie*, December.

Roeland Ordelman, Franciska de Jong, Arjan van Hessen, and Hendri Hondorp. 2007. TwNC: a multifaceted Dutch news corpus. *ELRA Newsletter*, 12(3/4):4–7.

Tanya Reinhart and Eric Reuland. 1993. Reflexivity. *Linguistic Inquiry*, 24:656–720.

Douglas Roland, Frederic Dick, and Jeffrey L. Elman. 2007. Frequency of basic english grammatical structures: A corpus analysis. *Journal of Memory and Language*, 57(3):348–379, October.

Erik-Jan Smits, Petra Hendriks, and Jennifer Spenader. 2007. Using very large parsed corpora and judgement data to classify verb reflexivity. In Antonio Branco, editor, *Anaphora: Analysis, Algorithms and Applications*, pages 77–93, Berlin. Springer.

Leonoor van der Beek, Gosse Bouma, and Gertjan van Noord. 2002. Een brede computationele grammatica voor het Nederlands. *Nederlandse Taalkunde*, 7(4):353–374.

Gertjan van Noord, Ineke Schuurman, and Vincent Vandeghinste. 2006. Syntactic annotation of large corpora in STEVIN. In *Proceedings of the 5th International Conference on Language Resources and Evaluation (LREC)*, Genoa, Italy.

Gertjan van Noord. 2006. **A**t **L**ast **P**arsing **I**s **N**ow **O**perational. In *TALN 2006 Verbum Ex Machina, Actes De La 13e Conference sur Le Traitement Automatique des Langues naturelles*, pages 20–42, Leuven.

Gertjan van Noord. 2009. Huge parsed corpora in Lassy. In Frank van Eynde, Anette Frank, Koenraad De Smedt, and Gertjan van Noord, editors, *Proceedings of the Seventh International Workshop on Treebanks and Linguistic Theories (TLT 7)*, number 12 in LOT Occasional Series, pages 115–126, Utrecht, The Netherlands. Netherlands Graduate School of Linguistics.

Annie Zaenen. 2004. but full parsing is impossible. *ELSNEWS*, 13(2):9–10.

Computational Linguistics and Linguistics:

What keeps them together, what sets them apart?

Gregor Erbach

Brussels, Belgium

gregor.erbach@gmail.com

Abstract

I will try to position the fields of Linguistics and Computational Linguistics by examining their objects of research, their objectives, approaches, and success criteria, drawing on the concepts shown in the text cloud below. This should give a clearer view of the commonalities, differences and potential synergies.

1 Concept Cloud[1]

---

[1] generated with Jonathan Feinberg's Wordle (IBM Research Visual Communication Lab)

Proceedings of the EACL 2009 Workshop on the Interaction between Linguistics and Computational Linguistics, page 40,
Athens, Greece, 30 March, 2009. ©2009 Association for Computational Linguistics

What Do Computational Linguists Need to Know about Linguistics?

Robert C. Moore
Microsoft Research
Redmond, Washington, USA
bobmoore@microsoft.com

Abstract

In this position paper, we argue that although the data-driven, empirical paradigm for computational linguistics seems to be the best way forward at the moment, a thorough grounding in descriptive linguistics is still needed to do competent work in the field. Examples are given of how knowledge of linguistic phenomena leads to understanding the limitations of particular statistical models and to better feature selection for such models.

Over the last twenty years, the field of computational linguistics has undergone a dramatic shift in focus from hand encoding linguistic facts in computer-oriented formalisms to applying statistical analysis and machine learning techniques to large linguistic corpora. Speaking as someone who has worked with both approaches, I believe that this change has been largely for the good, but I do not intend to argue that point here. Instead, I wish to consider what computational linguists (if it is still appropriate to call them that) need to know about linguistics, in order to work most productively within the current data-driven paradigm.

My view is that, while computational linguists may not need to know the details of particular linguistic theories (e.g., minimalism, LFG, HPSG), they do need to have an extensive understanding of the phenomena of language at a descriptive level. I can think of at least two somewhat distinct applications of this sort of knowledge in empirical computational linguistics.

One application is to understand the structural limitations of particular types of statistical models. For example, a descriptive generalization about language is that coordinated structures tend to be interpreted in such a way as to maximize structural parallelism. Thus, in the phrase "young men and women", "young" would normally be interpreted as applying to both "men" and "women", but in the phrase "young men and intelligent women", "young" would normally be interpreted as applying only to "men". Although both interpretations are structurally possible for both phrases, the preferred interpretations are the ones that maximize structural parallelism. This is a phenomenon that is not describable in a general way in a simple statistical model in the form of a probabilistic context-free grammar (PCFG). We could enumerate many specific cases by making fine-grained distinctions in the nonterminals of the grammar, but the tendency to favor parallel coordinated structures in general would not be expressed. This is not necessarily fatal to successful engineering applications of PCFGs, but a competent computational linguist should understand what the limitations of the formalism are.

Let me give another example from the notoriously empirical field of statistical machine translation (SMT). At least some linguistic structure has been creeping back into SMT recently in the form of hierarchical translation models, many of which can be viewed as instances of synchronous probabilistic (or more generally, weighted) context-free grammars (SPCFGs). This approach seems quite promising, but since it is based on a bilingual version of PCFGs, not only does it share the limitations of monolingual PCFGs alluded to above, but it also has additional structural limitations in the kind of generalizations over types of bilingual mappings it can model.

My favorite example of such a limitation is the translation of constituent (i.e., "WH") questions between languages that move questioned constituents to the front of the question ("WH-movement") and those that leave the questioned constituents *in situ*. English is an example of the former type of language, and Chinese (so I am told) is an example of the latter. If we wanted to make a model of question translation from Chi-

Proceedings of the EACL 2009 Workshop on the Interaction between Linguistics and Computational Linguistics, pages 41–42,
Athens, Greece, 30 March, 2009.

nese to English, we would like it to represent in a unitary (or at least finitary) way the generalization, "Translate the questioned constituent from Chinese to English and move it to the front of the English sentence being constructed." This generalization cannot be expressed in an SPCFG, because this type of model allows reordering to take place only among siblings of the same parent in the constituent structure. Fronting a questioned constituent, however, typically requires moving an embedded constituent up several levels in the constituent structure. While we can express specific instances of this type of movement using an SPCFG by flattening the intervening structure, we cannot hope to capture the generalization in full because WH-movement in English is famously unbounded, as in "What translation formalism did Moore claim to show that WH-movement could not be modeled in?"

In addition to providing a basis for understanding the limitations of what phenomena various statistical models can capture, a good knowledge of descriptive linguistics is also very useful as a source of features in statistical models. A good example of this comes from acoustic modeling in speech recognition. Acoustic models in speech recognition are typically composed of sequences of "phone" models, where a phone corresponds approximately to the linguistic unit of a phoneme. For good recognition performance, however, phone models need to be contextualized according to the other phones around them. Commonly, "triphone" models are used, in which a separate model is used for each combination of the phone preceding and following the phone being modeled. This can require over 100000 distinct models, depending on how many triphones are possible in a given language, which creates a sparse data problem for statistical estimation, since many of the possible combinations are only rarely observed.

One response to this sparse data problem is to cluster the states of the triphone models to reduce the number of separate models that need to be estimated, and an effective way to do this is to use decision trees. Using a decision tree clustering procedure, the set of all possible triphones is recursively split on relevant features of the triphone. At each decision point, the feature chosen for splitting is the one that produces the greatest improvement in the resulting model. But what features should be used in such a decision tree? I once heard a leading speech recognition engineer say that he chose his feature set by including all the features he could find in the linguistic phonetics literature. Given that feature set, the decision tree learning procedure decided which ones to actually use, and in what order.

The examples presented above illustrate some of the kinds of linguistic knowledge that a competent computational linguist needs to know in order perform research at the highest level. I am concerned that many of the students currently graduating in the field do not seem to have received sufficient exposure to the structure of language at this level of detail. For instance, a few years ago I pointed out the problem of modeling question translation between Chinese and English to one of the brightest young researchers working with SPCFGs, and the problem had never occurred to him, even though he was a fluent speaker of both languages. I am sure this would be one of the first things that would occur to anyone brought up on the debates of the 1980s about the limitations of context-free grammar, upon first exposure to the SPCFG formalism. So, although I am a firm believer that the data-driven empirical approach computational linguistics will remain the most fruitful research paradigm for the foreseeable future, I also think that researchers need a firm grounding in descriptive linguistics.

The Interaction of Syntactic Theory and Computational Psycholinguistics

Frank Keller
School of Informatics, University of Edinburgh
10 Crichton Street, Edinburgh EH8 9AB, UK
keller@inf.ed.ac.uk

1 Introduction

Typically, current research in psycholinguistics does not rely heavily on results from theoretical linguistics. In particular, most experimental work studying human sentence processing makes very straightforward assumptions about sentence structure; essentially only a simple context-free grammar is assumed. The main text book in psycholinguistics, for instance, mentions Minimalism in its chapter on linguistic description (Harley, 2001, ch. 2), but does not provide any details, and all the examples in this chapter, as well as in the chapters on sentence processing and language production (Harley, 2001, chs. 9, 12), only use context-free syntactic structures with uncontroversial phrase markers (S, VP, NP, etc.). The one exception is traces, which the textbook discusses in the context of syntactic ambiguity resolution.

Harley's (2001) textbook is typical of experimental psycholinguistics, a field in which most of the work is representationally agnostic, i.e., assumptions about syntactic structure left implicit, or limited to uncontroversial ones. However, the situation is different in computational psycholinguistics, where researchers built computationally implemented models of human language processing. This typically involves making one's theoretical assumptions explicit, a prerequisite for being able to implement them. For example, Crocker's (1996) model explicitly implements assumptions from the Principles and Parameters framework, while Hale (2006) uses probabilistic Minimalist grammars, or Mazzei et al. (2007) tree-adjoining grammars.

Here, we will investigate how evidence regarding human sentence processing can inform our assumptions about syntactic structure, at least in so far as this structure is used in computational models of human parsing.

2 Prediction and Incrementality

Evidence from psycholinguistic research suggests that language comprehension is largely *incremental*, i.e., that comprehenders build an interpretation of a sentence on a word-by-word basis. Evidence for incrementality comes from speech shadowing, self-paced reading, and eye-tracking studies (Marslen-Wilson, 1973; Konieczny, 2000; Tanenhaus et al., 1995): as soon as a reader or listener perceives a word in a sentence, they integrate it as fully as possible into a representation of the sentence thus far. They experience differential processing difficulty during this integration process, depending on the properties of the word and its relationship to the preceding context.

There is also evidence for full *connectivity* in human language processing (Sturt and Lombardo, 2005). Full connectivity means that all words are connected by a single syntactic structure; the parser builds no unconnected tree fragments, even for the incomplete sentences (sentence prefixes) that arise during incremental processing.

Furthermore, there is evidence that readers or listeners make *predictions* about upcoming material on the basis of sentence prefixes. Listeners can predict an upcoming post-verbal element, depending on the semantics of the preceding verb (Kamide et al., 2003). Prediction effects can also be observed in reading. Staub and Clifton (2006) showed that following the word *either* readers predict the conjunction *or* and the complement that follows it; processing was facilitated compared to structures that include *or* without *either*. In an ERP study, van Berkum et al. (1999) found that listeners use contextual information to predict specific lexical items and experience processing difficulty if the input is incompatible with the prediction.

The concepts of incrementality, connectedness, and prediction are closely related: in order to guar-

Proceedings of the EACL 2009 Workshop on the Interaction between Linguistics and Computational Linguistics, pages 43–46,
Athens, Greece, 30 March, 2009.

antee that the syntactic structure of a sentence prefix is fully connected, it may be necessary to build phrases whose lexical anchors (the words that they relate to) have not been encountered yet. Full connectedness is required to ensure that a fully interpretable structure is available at any point during incremental sentence processing.

Here, we explore how these key psycholinguistic concepts (incrementality, connectedness, and prediction) can be realized within a new version of tree-adjoining grammar, which we call Psycholinguistically Motivated TAG (PLTAG). We propose a formalization of PLTAG and a linking theory that derives predictions of processing difficulty from it. We then present an implementation of this model and evaluate it against key experimental data relating to incrementality and prediction. This approach is described in more detail in Demberg and Keller (2008) and Demberg and Keller (2009).

3 Modeling Explicit Prediction

We propose a theory of sentence processing guided by the principles of incrementality, connectedness, and prediction. The core assumption of our proposal is that a sentence processor that maintains explicit predictions about the upcoming structure has to validate these predictions against the input it encounters. Using this assumption, we can naturally combine the forward-looking aspect of Hale's (2001) surprisal (sentence structures are computed incrementally and unexpected continuations cause difficulty) with the backward-looking integration view of Gibson's (1998) dependency locality theory (previously predicted structures are verified against new evidence, leading to processing difficulty as predictions decay with time).

In order to build a model that implements this theory, we require an incremental parser that is capable of building fully connected structures and generating explicit predictions from which we can then derive a measure of processing difficulty. Existing parsers and grammar formalism do not meet this specification. While there is substantial previous work on incremental parsing, none of the existing model observes full connectivity. One likely reason for this is that full connectivity cannot be achieved using canonical linguistic structures as assumed in standard grammar formalisms such as CFG, CCG, TAG, LFG, or HPSG. Instead, a stack has to be used to store partial structures and retrieve them later when it has become clear (through additional input) how to combine them.

We therefore propose a new variant of the tree-adjoining grammar (TAG) formalism which realizes full connectedness. The key idea is that in cases where new input cannot be combined immediately with the existing structure, we need to predict additional syntactic material, which needs to be verified against future input later on.

4 Incremental Processing with PLTAG

PLTAG extends normal LTAG in that it specifies not only the canonical lexicon containing lexicalized initial and auxiliary trees, but also a predictive lexicon which contains potentially unlexicalized trees, which we will call *prediction trees*. Each node in a prediction tree is annotated with indices of the form $^{s_j}_{s_j}$, where inner nodes have two identical indices, root nodes only have a lower index and foot and substitution nodes only have an upper index. The reason for only having half of the indices is that these nodes (root, foot, and substitution nodes) still need to combine with another tree in order to build a full node. If an initial tree substitutes into a substitution node, the node where they are integrated becomes a full node, with the upper half contributed by the substitution node and the lower half contributed by the root node.

Prediction trees have the same shape as trees from the normal lexicon, with the difference that they do not contain substitution nodes to the right of their spine (the spine is the path from the root node to the anchor), and that their spine does not have to end with a lexical item. The reason for the missing right side of the spine and the missing lexical item are considerations regarding the granularity of prediction. This way, for example, we avoid predicting verbs with specific subcategorization frames (or even a specific verb). In general, we only predict upcoming structure as far as we need it, i.e., as required by connectivity or subcategorization. (However, this is a preliminary assumption, the optimal prediction grain size remains an open research question.)

PLTAG allows the same basic operations (substitution and adjunction) as normal LTAG, the only difference is that these operations can also be applied to prediction trees. In addition, we assume a verification operation, which is needed to validate previously integrated prediction trees. The tree against which verification happens has to always match the predicted tree in shape (i.e., the verification tree must contain all the nodes with a unique, identical index that were present in the prediction tree, and in the same order; any additional nodes present in the verification tree must be below the prediction tree anchor or to the right of its spine). This means that the verification operation does not introduce any tree configurations that would not be allowed by normal LTAG. Note that substitution or adjunction with a predictive tree and the verification of that tree always occur pairwise, since each predicted node has to be verified. A valid parse for a sentence must not contain any nodes that are still annotated as being predictive – all of them have to be validated through verification by the end of the sentence.

5 Modeling Processing Difficulty

Our variant of TAG is designed to implement a specific set of assumptions about human language processing (strong incrementality with full connectedness, prediction, ranked parallel processing). The formalism forms the basis for the processing theory, which uses the parser states to derive estimates of processing difficulty. In addition, we need a linking theory that specifies the mathematical relationship between parser states and processing difficulty in our model.

During processing, the elementary tree of each new word is integrated with any previous structure, and a set of syntactic expectations is generated (these expectations can be easily read off the generated tree in the form of predicted trees). Each of these predicted trees has a time-stamp that encodes when it was first predicted, or last activated (i.e., accessed). Based on the timestamp, a tree's decay at verification time is calculated, under the assumption that recently-accessed structures are easier to integrate.

In our model, processing difficulty is thus incurred during the construction of the syntactic analyses, as calculated from the probabilities of the elementary trees (this directly corresponds to Haleian surprisal calculated over PLTAG structures instead of over CFG structures). In addition to this, processing difficulty has a second component, the cost of verifying earlier predictions, which is subject to decay.

The verification cost component bears similarities to DLT integration costs, but we do not calculate distance in terms of number of discourse referents intervening between a dependent and its head. Rather verification cost is determined by the number of words intervening between a prediction and its verification, subject to decay. This captures the intuition that a prediction becomes less and less useful the longer ago it was made, as it decays from memory with increasing distance.

6 Evaluation

In Demberg and Keller (2009), we present an implementation of the PLTAG model, including a lexicon induction procedure, a parsing algorithm, and a probability model. We show that the resulting framework can capture experimental results from the literature, and can explain both locality and prediction effects, which standard models of sentence processing like DLT and surprisal are unable to account for simultaneously.

Our model therefore constitutes a step towards a unified theory of human parsing that potentially captures a broad range of experimental findings. This work also demonstrates that (computational) psycholinguistics cannot afford to be representationally agnostic – a comprehensive, computationally realistic theory of human sentence processing needs to make explicit assumptions about syntactic structure. Here, we showed how the fact that human parsing is incremental and predictive necessitates certain assumptions about syntactic structure (such as full connectedness), which can be implemented by augmenting an existing grammar formalism, viz., tree-adjoining grammar. Note, however, that it is difficult to show that this approach is the only one that is able to realize the required representational assumptions; other solutions using different grammar formalisms are presumably possible.

7 Acknowledgments

This abstract reports joint work with Vera Demberg, described in more detail in Demberg and Keller (2008) and Demberg and Keller (2009). The research was supported by EPSRC grant EP/C546830/1 Prediction in Human Parsing.

References

Crocker, Matthew W. 1996. *Computational Psycholinguistics: An Interdisciplinary Approach to the Study of Language*. Kluwer, Dordrecht.

Demberg, Vera and Frank Keller. 2008. A psycholinguistically motivated version of TAG. In

Proceedings of the 9th International Workshop on Tree Adjoining Grammars and Related Formalisms. Tübingen.

Demberg, Vera and Frank Keller. 2009. A computational model of prediction in human parsing: Unifying locality and surprisal effects. Manuscript under review.

Gibson, Edward. 1998. Linguistic complexity: locality of syntactic dependencies. *Cognition* 68:1–76.

Hale, John. 2001. A probabilistic Earley parser as a psycholinguistic model. In *Proceedings of the 2nd Conference of the North American Chapter of the Association for Computational Linguistics*. Association for Computational Linguistics, Pittsburgh, PA, volume 2, pages 159–166.

Hale, John. 2006. Uncertainty about the rest of the sentence. *Cognitive Science* 30(4):609–642.

Harley, Trevor. 2001. *The Psychology of Language: From Data to Theory*. Psychology Press,, Hove, 2 edition.

Kamide, Yuki, Christoph Scheepers, and Gerry T. M. Altmann. 2003. Integration of syntactic and semantic information in predictive processing: Cross-linguistic evidence from german and english. *Journal of Psycholinguistic Research* 32:37–55.

Konieczny, Lars. 2000. Locality and parsing complexity. *Journal of Psycholinguistic Research* 29(6):627–645.

Marslen-Wilson, William D. 1973. Linguistic structure and speech shadowing at very short latencies. *Nature* 244:522–523.

Mazzei, Alessandro, Vicenzo Lombardo, and Patrick Sturt. 2007. Dynamic TAG and lexical dependencies. *Research on Language and Computation* 5(3):309–332.

Staub, Adrian and Charles Clifton. 2006. Syntactic prediction in language comprehension: Evidence from either . . . or. *Journal of Experimental Psychology: Learning, Memory, and Cognition* 32:425–436.

Sturt, Patrick and Vincenzo Lombardo. 2005. Processing coordinated structures: Incrementality and connectedness. *Cognitive Science* 29(2):291–305.

Tanenhaus, Michael K., Michael J. Spivey-Knowlton, Kathleen M. Eberhard, and Julie C. Sedivy. 1995. Integration of visual and linguistic information in spoken language comprehension. *Science* 268:1632–1634.

van Berkum, J. J. A., C. M. Brown, and Peter Hagoort. 1999. Early referential context effects in sentence processing: Evidence from event-related brain potentials. *Journal of Memory and Language* 41:147–182.